IB ECONOMICS

PAPER 3 : Practice Questions with Detailed Answers

Kelvin Hong

First Printing: 2016

ISBN 978-981-11-0295-0

Edventures Pte Ltd

Singapore

www.TheEconomicsTutor.com

Acknowledgments

This work would not have been possible without the valuable help of Wilson Lim Yew Phern.

PREFACE

This book addresses many possible questions across the entire IB Economics syllabus pertaining to the Paper 3 examinations. There are 3 sections – Microeconomics, Macroeconomics and International Trade.

Very often, students are unable to apply the economics concepts to solve the mathematical problem sums because of a lack of understanding of the economics concepts and theories in the first place. By provide step-by-step workings and explanations, this book will provide a rigorous practice to help students build up both their understanding of the economics concepts and mathematical problem solving skills.

I hope that this book will help all students better appreciate what they are learning and excel in their economics examinations.

Kelvin Hong

CONTENTS

Part 1 – Microeconomics

Section A – Demand and Supply

1) The demand and supply functions for chicken rice are:

$Qd = 18 - 2P$ and

$Qs = 6P - 6$ respectively,

where Qd and Qs are quantities in hundreds of plates and P is the price per plate in dollars ($).

    a) Fill in the Qd and Qs columns in the following table.   [2m]

Price ($ per plate)	Qd (hundred plates)	Qs (hundred plates)
1		
2		
3		
4		
5		

b) Plot and label the functions using the table of values calculated above.   [2m]

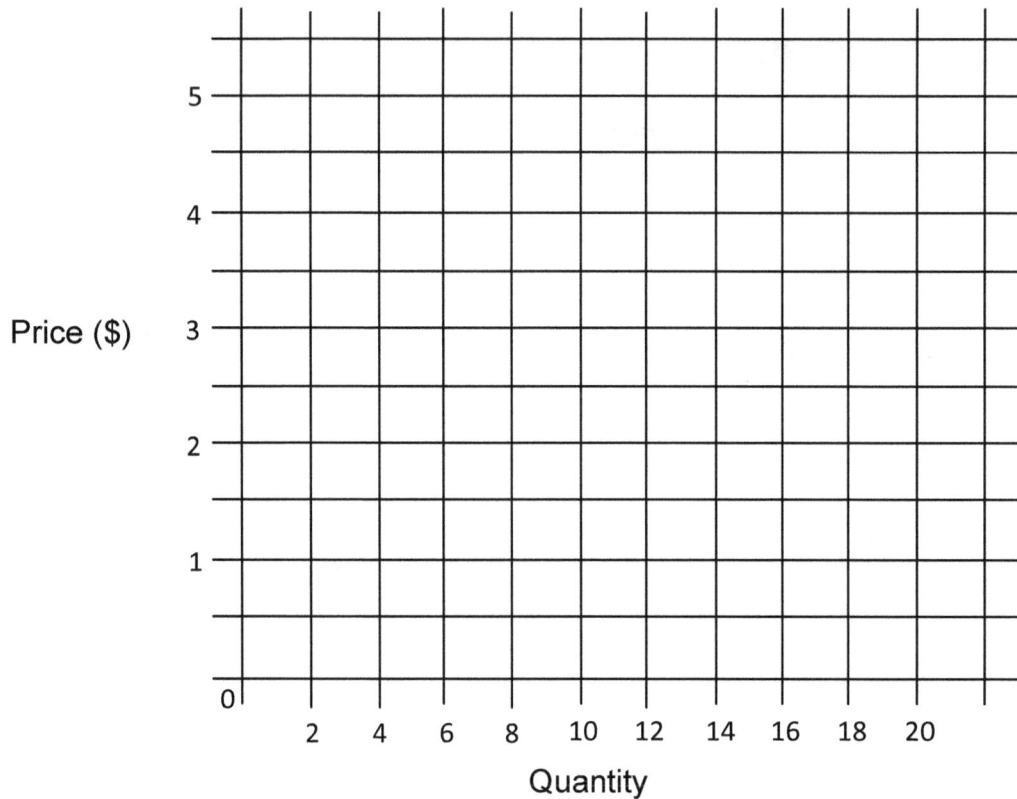

c) Calculate, using algebra, the equilibrium price and quantity implied by the intersection of the two functions. Check that it agrees with what is suggested by your graph from part (b).   [2m]

ii) Find the consumer and producer surplus enjoyed at this equilibrium point.

[2m]

The government then decides to implement a price floor of $4 for the market of chicken rice.

d) i) Would there be a shortage or surplus in response and of how many units?

[2m]

ii) If the government decides to buy any quantity not sold in the market, what would be the total cost required? [2m]

e) Compare the producer revenue and consumer expenditure in this situation (the $4 price floor) with the producer revenue and consumer expenditure in the initial situation without the price floor. [3m]

f) i) Calculate the consumer and producer surplus enjoyed at this point (after the $4 price floor) [3m]

ii) Has the price floor transferred some surplus from consumers to producers and if so, how much? [2m]

iii) Has some welfare simply been lost? If so, shade the area of the welfare loss on the graph in (b) and calculate the extent of the welfare loss. [3m]

2) The following table shows the daily supply and demand functions for good Y.

Qd	Price in $	Qs
60	4.50	105
70	4.00	100
80	3.50	95
90	3.00	90
100	2.50	85
110	2.00	80
120	1.50	75

a) From the table of values, derive the demand and supply functions in the form of an equation Q = A + BP, where Q is the quantity of units, A and B are arbitrary constants while P is the price of each unit. [4m]

b) Plot and label the demand and supply functions using the table of values above then identify the equilibrium price and quantity from the graph drawn.

[3m]

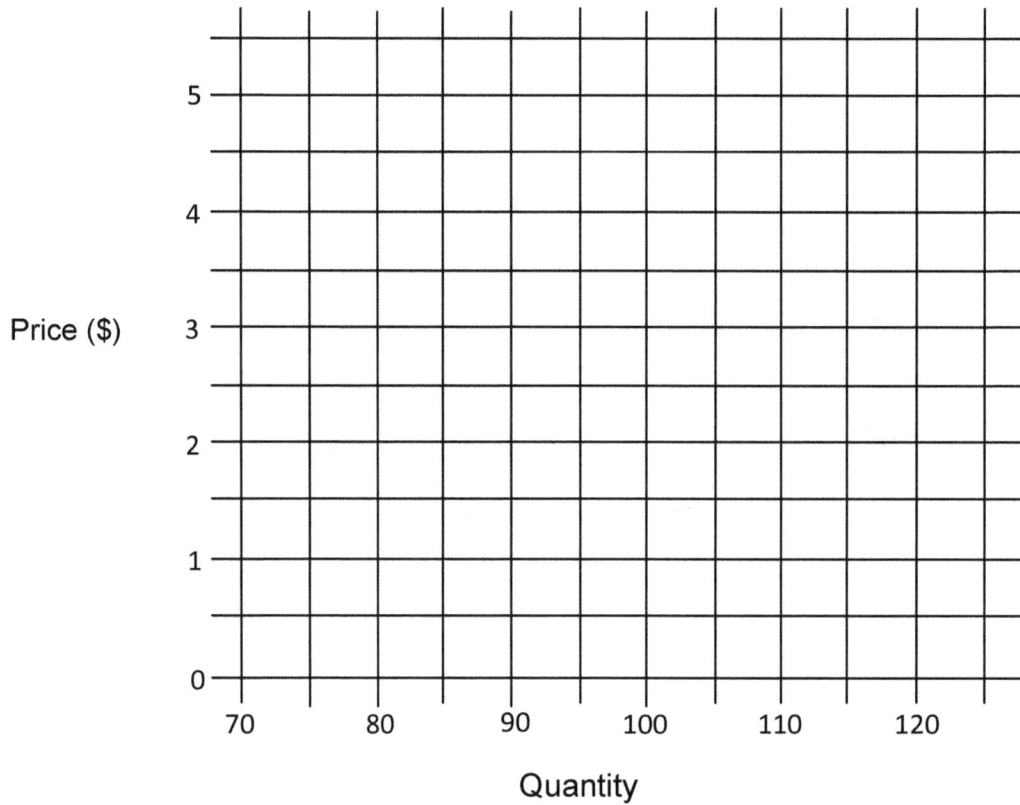

c) Calculate the price elasticity of demand for an increase in price from $3 per unit to $3.50 per unit. [2m]

d) From the two equations in (a),

i) How can you tell how many units consumers would want to buy at a price of zero? [1m]

ii) At what price would the producers supply the quantity of goods as calculated in (di)? [2m]

e) If the demand for good Y becomes relatively more price elastic in the long run, what would happen to the quantity demanded when its price increases? [2m]

Recently, good X, a substitute for good Y, has been newly launched into the market.

f) Would a decrease in the price of good X cause an increase or decrease in the demand of good Y. Why? [2m]

Assuming that a decrease in the price of good X caused the demand for good Y to decrease by 30 units at all prices.

g) State the equation for the new demand function. [2m]

h) Find the new equilibrium price and quantity. [2m]

3) The following diagram shows the market for handbags.

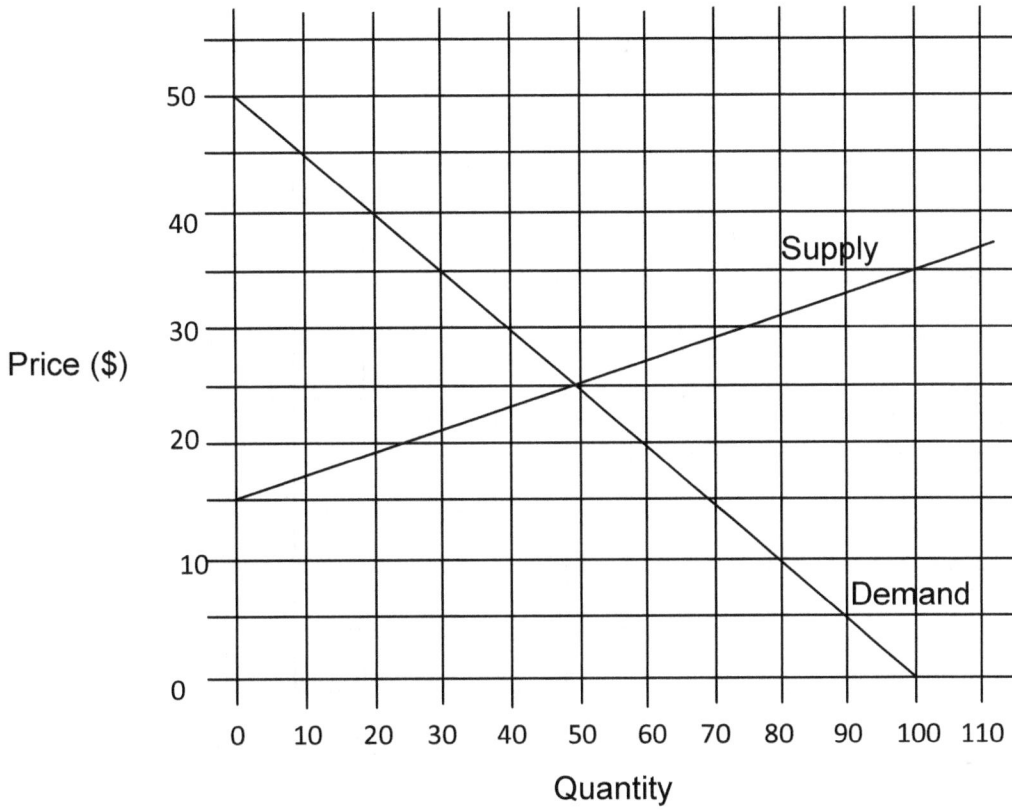

a) Calculate the consumer and producer surplus from the diagram above.   [2m]

b) Copy the above diagram and apply a specific indirect tax of $5 per unit to the handbags. Plot the resultant supply and demand curves on the same diagram.

[2m]

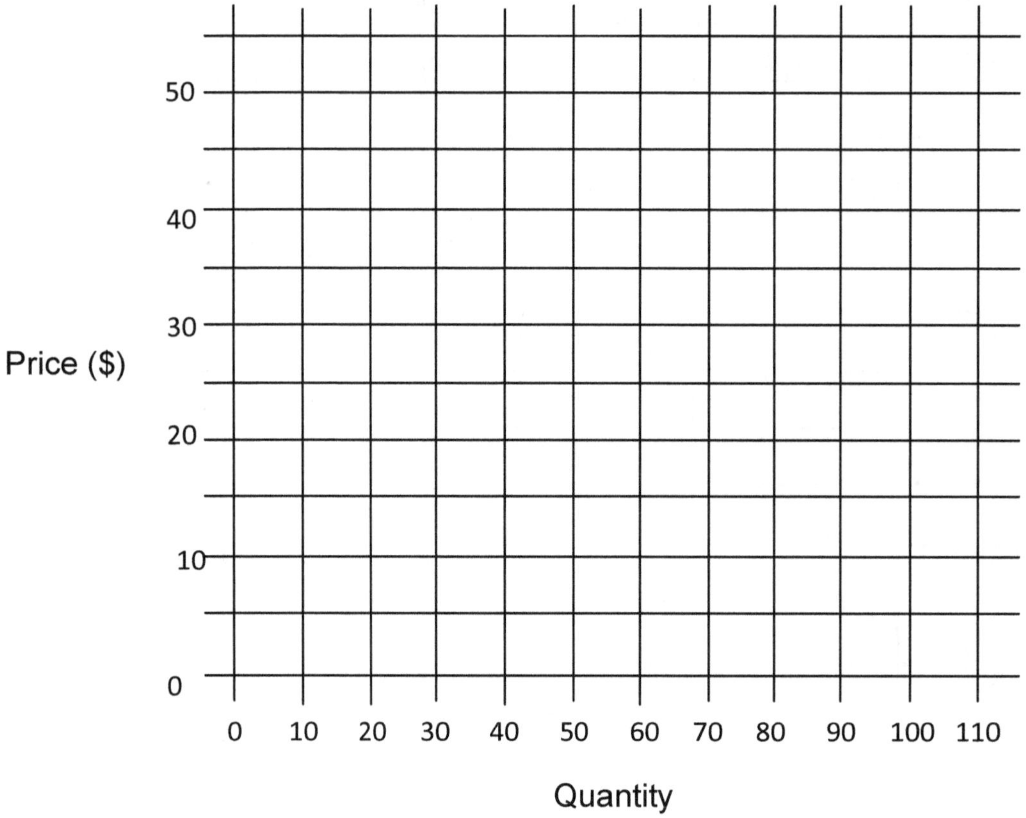
Price ($)
50
40
30
20
10
0
0
10
20
30
40
50
60
70
80
90
100
110
Quantity

c) Using the graph drawn in (b), determine the new equilibrium price and quantity. Hence, calculate the total tax revenue to the government. [5m]

d) Calculate the new consumer and producer surplus after the tax has been implemented. [2m]

e) By considering the sum of the post-tax consumer and producer surplus and the tax revenue to the government, as well as the sum of the consumer and producer surplus before the tax was implemented, what has been the impact of the tax on the overall welfare? [3m]

4) Given the same linear demand and supply functions as were used in question 3

a) Calculate the consumer expenditure and producer revenue from the diagram.

[2m]

b) Copy the diagram and apply a specific indirect subsidy of $5 per unit to the handbags. Plot the resultant supply and demand curves on the same diagram.

[2m]

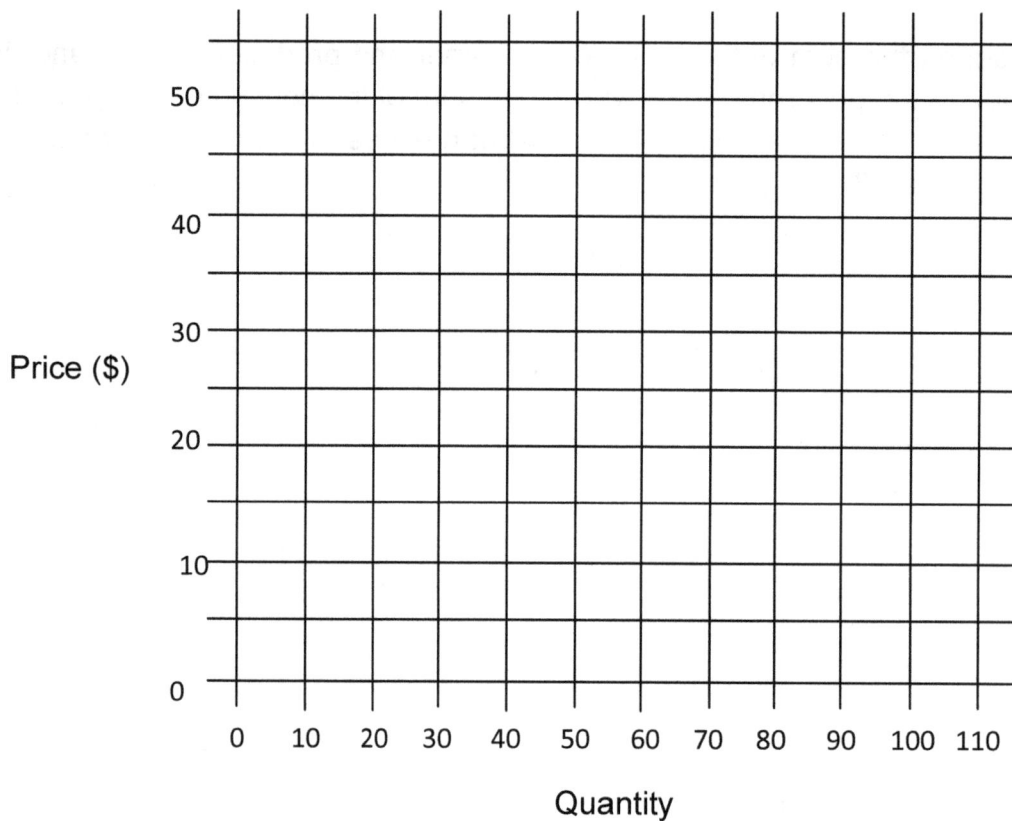

Price ($)

Quantity

c) Determine the new equilibrium price and quantity. [3m]

d) i) Calculate the consumer expenditure and producer revenue after the subsidy was applied. [2m]

   ii) After making necessary comparisons on both the consumer expenditure and producer revenue before and after the subsidy, determine the impact of the subsidy on each. [2m]

e) i) Calculate the incidence of the subsidy on both the consumer and producer. [3m]

   ii) Who benefited more from the subsidy? Explain why this is so. [2m]

Part 1 – Microeconomics

Section B – Market structure

1) A farmer has a fixed amount of land and workers. However, he can vary the number of harvesters he uses. He finds that his total production of papayas varies with the number of harvesters he uses as described by the table below:

Number of harvesters	Output of papayas (tonnes)	Marginal Output (tonnes)	Average Output (tonnes)
0	10		
1	25		
2	46		
3	69		
4	88		
5	100		
6	107		
7	110		
8	110		

a) Copy the table above and,

i) Calculate the marginal output of each additional harvester. [2m]

ii) Calculate the average output attributable to each harvester for all quantities of harvesters. [2m]

Number of harvesters	Output of papayas (tonnes)	Marginal Output (tonnes)	Average Output (tonnes)
0	10		
1	25		
2	46		
3	69		
4	88		
5	100		
6	107		
7	110		
8	110		

b) At what point does the farmer begin suffering diminishing returns from using additional harvesters? [2m]

Assume that each harvester cost $6000 to purchase and operate while papaya prices are $500 per tonne.

c) Calculate the total cost of producing 100 tonnes of papayas. [2m]

d) Calculate the value of papayas produced by the 6th harvested. [2m]

e) i) How many harvesters should the farmer use to maximise his returns? Explain your answer. [3m]

ii) What would be the total profit if the farmer decides to employ that number of harvesters as calculated above in e) i)? [2m]

Assume that a 15% tax was introduced on the farmer's profit.

f) How would this affect his profit maximising output? [1m]

g) Calculate the new level of profit as well as the government revenue from the tax. [3m]

2) The following table shows the daily output of an online store which sells electronic gadgets.

Output	Total Costs ($)	Marginal Costs ($)	Average costs ($)	Total Revenue ($)	Marginal Revenue ($)	Average Revenue ($)
0	20			0		
1	30			24		
2	38			44		
3	44			60		
4	48			72		
5	50			80		
6	54			84		
7	60			84		
8	68			80		
9	78			72		
10	90			60		

a) From the table above, what are the store's fixed costs? Explain your answer.

[2m]

b) Thus, calculate the average variable cost where output is 5 units.   [2m]

c) Copy the table above and,

i) Calculate the store's marginal and average cost [2m]
ii) As well as marginal and average revenue, at each level of output. [2m]

Output	Total Costs ($)	Marginal Costs ($)	Average costs ($)	Total Revenue ($)	Marginal Revenue ($)	Average Revenue ($)
0	20			0		
1	30			24		
2	38			44		
3	44			60		
4	48			72		
5	50			80		
6	54			84		
7	60			84		
8	68			80		
9	78			72		
10	90			60		

d) For 4 units of output,

   i) Find the average fixed costs,   [2m]

   ii) And the average variable costs.   [2m]

e) i) Calculate the store's profit maximising output.   [4m]

   ii) Find the total profit at that point and determine the type of profit.   [3m]

f) What would be the store's revenue-maximizing output?   [2m]

g) What would you expect to happen in this market in the long run and how
    would it affect the store's pricing and output decisions.   [2m]

h) i) On the grid below, plot the store's marginal and average costs curves as well as marginal and average revenue curves. [4m]

ii) On the graphs plotted, mark in the profit maximising and revenue maximising points as A and B respectively. [2m]

Costs/ Revenue ($)

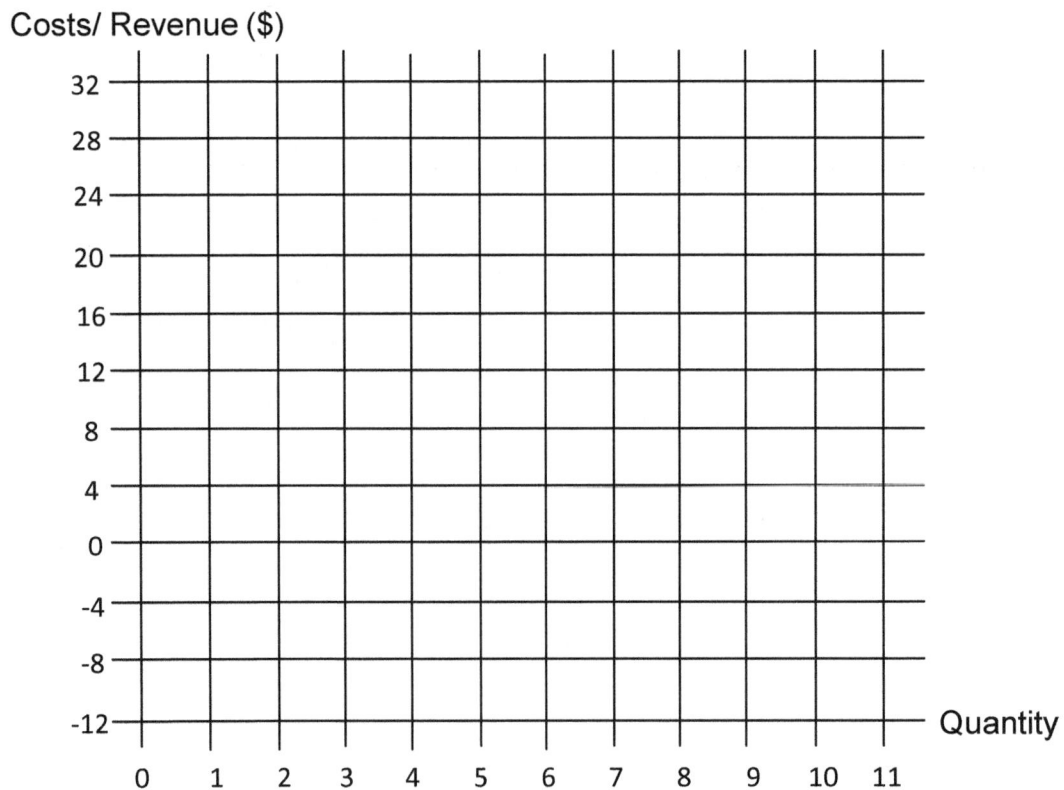

3) A cookie manufacturer exhibits the following costs and revenue in the table below.

Quantity of cookies	Total costs($)	Variable costs($)	Marginal costs($)	Average variable costs($)	Average total costs($)	Total revenue ($)	Marginal revenue ($)
0	0.5					0	
1	3					5	
2	4.5					9.5	
3	6.5					13.5	
4	9					17	
5	12					20	
6	15.5					22.5	
7	19.5					24.5	
8	24					26	

a) Copy and complete the table above after calculating the relevant costs and revenues. [5m]

Quantity of cookies	Total costs($)	Variable costs($)	Marginal costs($)	Average variable costs($)	Average total costs($)	Total revenue ($)	Marginal revenue ($)
0	0.5					0	
1	3					5	
2	4.5					9.5	
3	6.5					13.5	
4	9					17	
5	12					20	
6	15.5					22.5	
7	19.5					24.5	
8	24					26	

b) i) At what price would each cookie be sold at if 5 cookies were produced? [2m]

ii) What is the profit from each cookie? [2m]

c) Determine the profit maximising output and price for the cookie manufacturer.

[4m]

d) If the fixed costs for the cookie manufacturer were to double, how would the profit maximizing price and quantity be affected? Why? [2m]

e) Is this pie seller operating in a perfectly competitive market? Explain your answer. [2m]

f) i) At which level of output are average variable costs at a minimum? [1m]

ii) What is likely to happen if the selling price of the manufacturer's cookie is below this minimum amount? [2m]

iii) What is likely to happen if the selling price of the manufacturer's cookie is above the minimum average variable cost but below the minimum average total cost? [2m]

g) If the market price for cookies increased to $4, calculate the new profit maximising output and new level of profit. [4m]

h) Calculate the PED necessary for a price change to increase the quantity of cookies sold from 4 to 6. [4m]

4) A monopolist supplies a product with a demand curve following an equation of $2\ Qd = 20 - P$. The marginal cost for the product is $6 while the fixed cost is at $ 10.

Price ($)	20	18	16	14	12	10	8	6	4
Qd									
Total Revenue ($)									
Marginal Revenue ($)									
Average revenue ($)									

a) Complete the table above after calculating the relevant quantities and revenues. [4m]

b) i) On the grid below, plot the monopolist's marginal cost curve, along with the marginal and average revenue curves. [3m]

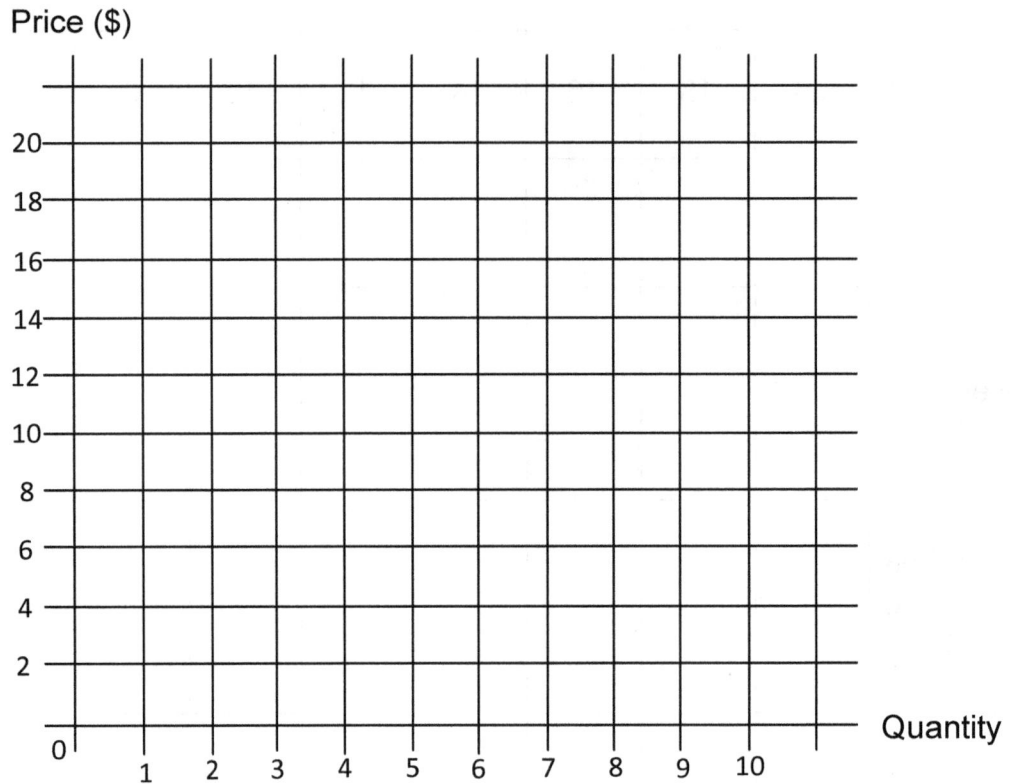

Price ($)

```
20
18
16
14
12
10
 8
 6
 4
 2
 0
    1  2  3  4  5  6  7  8  9  10        Quantity
```

ii) Identify the point on the graph which is allocative efficient and label the point, A. Explain your answer. [2m]

iii) How would the allocative efficient price affect the monopolist's profitability? [2m]

c) i) Calculate the profit maximising output and price for the monopolist, as well as the maximum profit. [5m]

ii) Label the profit maximising point on the graph drawn in (b) as B. [2m]

d) From the graph, calculate the producer and consumer surplus,

i) At the allocative efficient point, A. [2m]

ii) At the profit maximising point, B. [2m]

iii) How much surplus was transferred from consumers to the monopolist, and how much became the deadweight loss. [3m]

In order to limit the welfare loss due to monopoly, the government decides to implement a specific indirect tax of $4 for every unit of the product.

e) Calculate the new producer and consumer surplus after the tax and calculate the new extent of the welfare loss to determine whether or not the tax would achieve the government's aim. [4m]

f) If the marginal cost becomes zero, what would be the new profit maximising price? [2m]

Part 2 – Macroeconomics

1) The following information relates to the economy of Country Y.

Annual expenditure	Billion dollars ($bn)
Consumption (C)	45
Investment (I)	12.5
Government Spending (G)	20
Exports (X)	7.5
Imports (M)	10

Capital consumption = $5bn

Net Property Income from Abroad = – $2.5bn

MPC = 0.5   **MPS = 0.2**

MPT = 0.2   **MPM = 0.1**

a) Calculate the Gross Domestic Product (GDP) of country Y.   [2m]

b) Find out the Net National Product of country Y. How would it be different from that
    of the GDP value?   [2m]

c) What is the total value of injections into Country Y?   [2m]

d) Calculate the total value of withdrawals in order for the Income of the country to be
    in equilibrium.   [2m]

e) Calculate the external deficit as a percentage of GDP for country Y.   [2m]

Assume that the government decides to increase their spending from $20bn to $25bn as a result of the building of additional infrastructures in the country.

f) Find out the value of the multiplier. [2m]

g) Calculate the new equilibrium level of income. [2m]

h) What would be the new value of Consumption? [2m]

i) Calculate the new value of Imports. [2m]

2) The values of Income (Y), Consumption (C), Savings(S) and Investment (I) for a closed economy with no government sector are presented in the table below.

Y ($million)	C ($million)	S ($million)	I ($million)
0	100		20
50	130		20
100	160		20
150	190		20
200	220		20
250	250		20
300	280		20
350	310		20
400	340		20
450	370		20
500	400		20

a) Complete the table above by filling in the S column.   [2m]

b) Find the equilibrium level of income.   [2m]

c) Calculate the value of MPC and MPS for this economy.   [2m]

d) At what level of income is the Average Propensity to Consume = 1.   [2m]

e) Calculate the value of the multiplier.   [2m]

Assume that the Investments are increased to 80 at each level of Income.

   f)   Find the new equilibrium level of income.   [2m]

   g)   If full employment is at Y = 500, calculate the size of the deflationary gap.   [2m]

   h)   Determine the increase in investment level necessary to close the deflationary gap calculated in (g).   [2m]

3) The following information relates to the economy of country X from the year 2005 to 2015.

For 2005 and 2010, the economy only produced toiletries, utensils and stationaries.

Products	Output for 2005	Output for 2010	Price for 2005 ($ per unit)	Price for 2010 ($ per unit)
Toiletries	100	200	2	3
Utensils	100	250	3	4
Stationaries	100	140	1	1.5

a) Calculate the nominal GDP in country X in 2005 and 2010. [2m]

b) What was the nominal rate of economic growth between 2005 and 2010? [2m]

c) Find out the real GDP in 2010 at 2005 prices. [4m]

d) Calculate the percentage increase in real GDP from 2005 to 2010. [2m]

e) Explain the difference between the real and nominal GDP growth from 2005 to 2010 for country X. [3m]

For 2015, the accounts of national expenditure are as follows:

- Consumption spending by households   = $100 billion
- Total investment spending by firms   = $15 billion
- Depreciation of firms' existing capital stock*   = $3 billion
- Government spending on goods and services   = $20 billion
- Import expenditure   = $30 billion
- Export revenue   = $31 billion

*Spending needed to replace worn out machinery and equipment.

f) Calculate the nominal GDP from the expenditure side for 2015.   [2m]

g) If country X has a national population of 23 million, what would be its nominal GDP per capita?   [2m]

h) If the country's GDP deflator was set at '100' in 2014 and was estimated to be '110' in 2015, what would be the country's real GDP in 2015, measured in constant 2014 dollars?   [2m]

i) If the country's workers and firms operating abroad produced and earned $10 billion while the workers and firms of other countries operating within the nation produced and earned $5 billion in 2015, what would be the nominal Gross National Product (GNP) for the country that year?   [2m]

4) The table below shows the employment figures for Country X from 2010 to 2014.

Year	Population of Working Age (millions)	Labour Force (millions)	Total Employment (millions)
2010	41	23	20.4
2011	42	23.6	21.2
2012	42.4	24.4	22.2
2013	43	25	22.4
2014	44	25.6	21.6

a) Calculate the number of workers unemployed in 2012 and 2014.　　　　[2m]

b) Find out the rate of unemployment as a percentage for all 5 years shown above. [4m]

c) If there were 400 000 job vacancies in 2014, what would be the most likely type of unemployment in the country? Explain your answer. [4m]

5) The following table shows the income tax regimes for Country X.

Country X	
Income Level	Tax rate (%)
First $15 000	0
$15 001 – $25 000	10
$25 001 – $35 000	20
$35 001 – $45 000	30
$45 001 – $55 000	40
$55 001 – $65 000	50
Above $65 000	60

Adam, Bill and Charles are planning to work in Country X. Based on their educational qualifications, Adam earns an annual income of $10 000, while Bill is able to earn $30 000 a year and Charles gets an $85 000 annual income.

a) What would be Bill and Charles' marginal rate of income tax?   [2m]

b) Calculate the tax that Adam, Bill and Charles each have to pay if all of them decide to work in Country X. [6m]

c) What are Bill and Charles' average income tax rate in country X? [2m]

The government then imposes an additional Value Added Tax (VAT) on all expenditure at a fixed rate of 18% for both countries. Adam, Bill and Charles spend a certain percentage of their income as follows:

Adam   – 50%

Bill   – 60%

Charles   – 45%

d) Taking into account all the information above, calculate the percentage of income paid in tax for Adam, Bill and Charles if they decide to work in Country X.   [9m]

e) If the income tax system in Country X changes so that everyone pays 25% tax regardless of income, and VAT becomes 20%, will the Gini coefficient for the country be larger or smaller than before?   [2m]

6) The following table shows the prices and weights of a representative sample of products used to calculate a retail price index.

Product	Price in 2010 ($)	Price in 2011 ($)	Price in 2012 ($)	Weight (%)
A	500	515	520	25
B	2	2	2	25
C	30	25	35	12.5
D	0.1	0.12	0.13	12.5
E	1	1.35	1.1	12.5
F	7	7.5	7	12.5

Assuming that 2010 is the base year so that the RPI is 100 in 2010:

a) Calculate a weighted price index for 2011.   [4m]

b) Calculate the average percentage increase in prices from 2010 to 2011.

[2m]

c) Explain the difference in your answer for (a) and (b) for the year 2011.

[2m]

d) If Alex spent $2000 on this sample of products in 2010, how much would she spend to buy the same sample of products in 2012? [2m]

If Bryan spends all his income on product A,

e) Calculate the percentage change in his real income between 2011 and 2012.

[3m]

f) If Bryan's real income in 2011 was represented by an index of 100, calculate the index (to the nearest whole number) that would represent his real income in 2012.

[2m]

7) The RPI for Country X is shown in the following table:

Year	2008	2009	2010	2011	2012	2013	2014	2015
RPI	97	100	101	103	102	99	97	93

a) Which year is the base year? [1m]

b) Calculate the rate of inflation for 2011. [2m]

c) In which year did Country X face the highest rate of inflation? [2m]

d) Were prices in 2008 higher than in 2015? Explain your answer. [2m]

e) Is Country X suffering from inflation, deflation or dis-inflation from 2011 to 2015? Explain your answer. [2m]

Part 3 – International Trade

1) The following diagram shows the German market for steel.

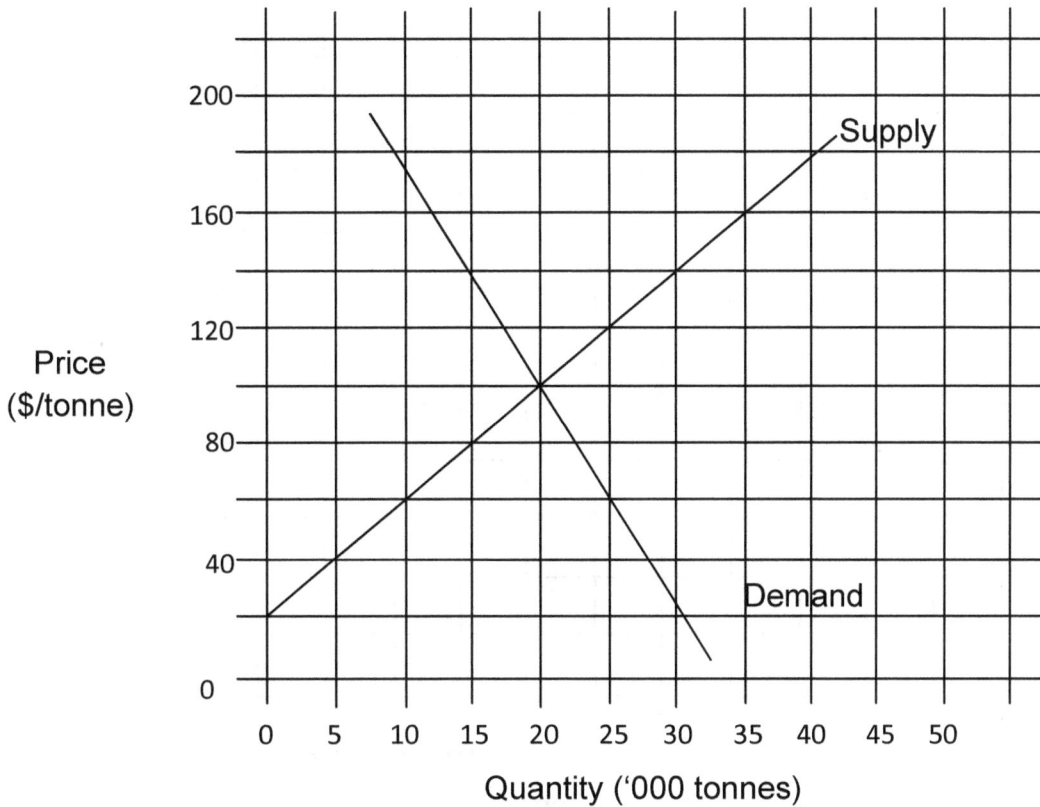

a) What is the equilibrium price and quantity in the above market?   [2m]

If Germany were to open its steel market to free trade, and suppliers in other countries were allowed to supply an unlimited quantity of steel at a price of $60 per tonne.

b) i) Copy the diagram above and make the necessary changes to reflect the entry of foreign suppliers into the German steel market. [2m]

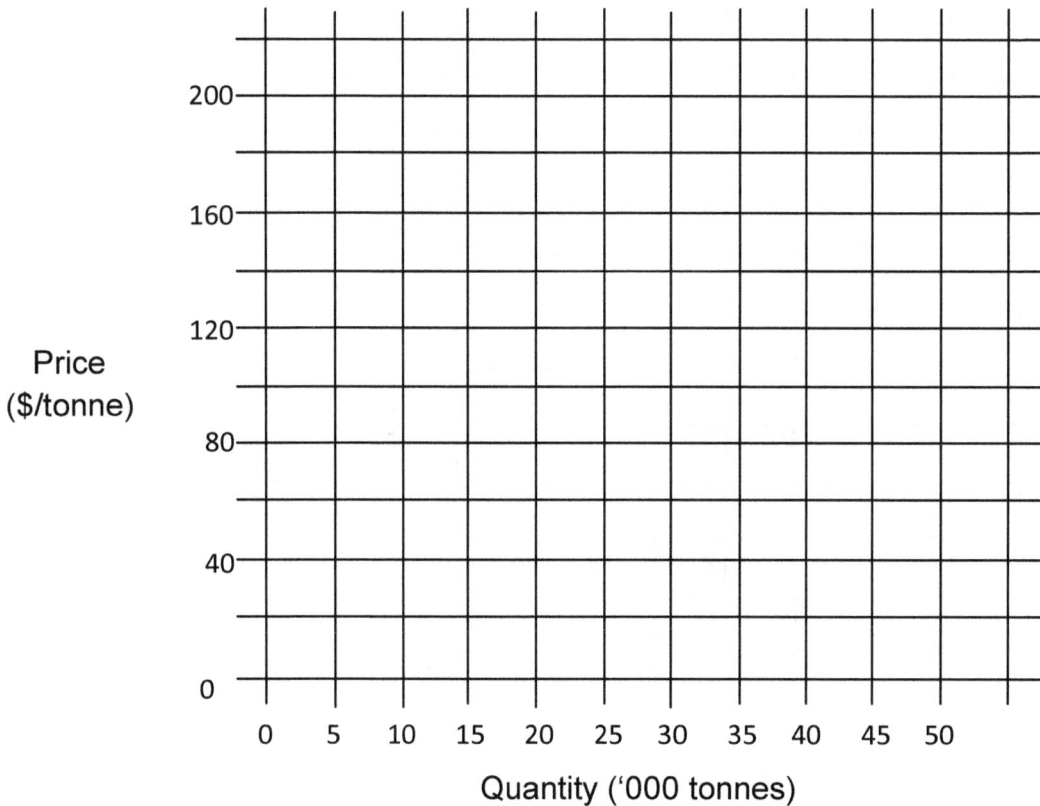

Price ($/tonne) vs Quantity ('000 tonnes)

ii) What would be the new equilibrium price and quantity at which steel is sold in Germany when foreign steel is made available for sale in the country? [2m]

c) i) How have the revenues of the domestic steel producers been affected by the entry of imported steel? Using the diagram drawn in part b) ii), compare their revenue before and after free trade was permitted.   [4m]

ii) How much revenue are the foreign steel suppliers earning from the local steel buyers in Germany?   [2m]

d) How has the producer surplus been affected by the entry of the imported steel? Calculate the producer surplus before and after free trade was made available.   [2m]

In order to protect the domestic steel producers, the German government decide to impose a $20 tariff on steel.

e) Reflect the tariff on the diagram drawn in part (bi) and find the new equilibrium price and quantity. [3m]

f) Determine the revenue for the government from the tariff they implemented. [2m]

g) Find the additional revenue earned by the domestic German steel producers and thus calculate the loss in revenue by the foreign steel suppliers in the German steel market. [4m]

Following the tariff from the government on imported steel, many complaints were received from the public saying that steel products are too expensive. Hence, the government decides to eliminate the tariff and replace it with an import quota of 7500 tonnes of steel.

h) Copy the original diagram and model the impact of the quota in the grid below.
[2m]

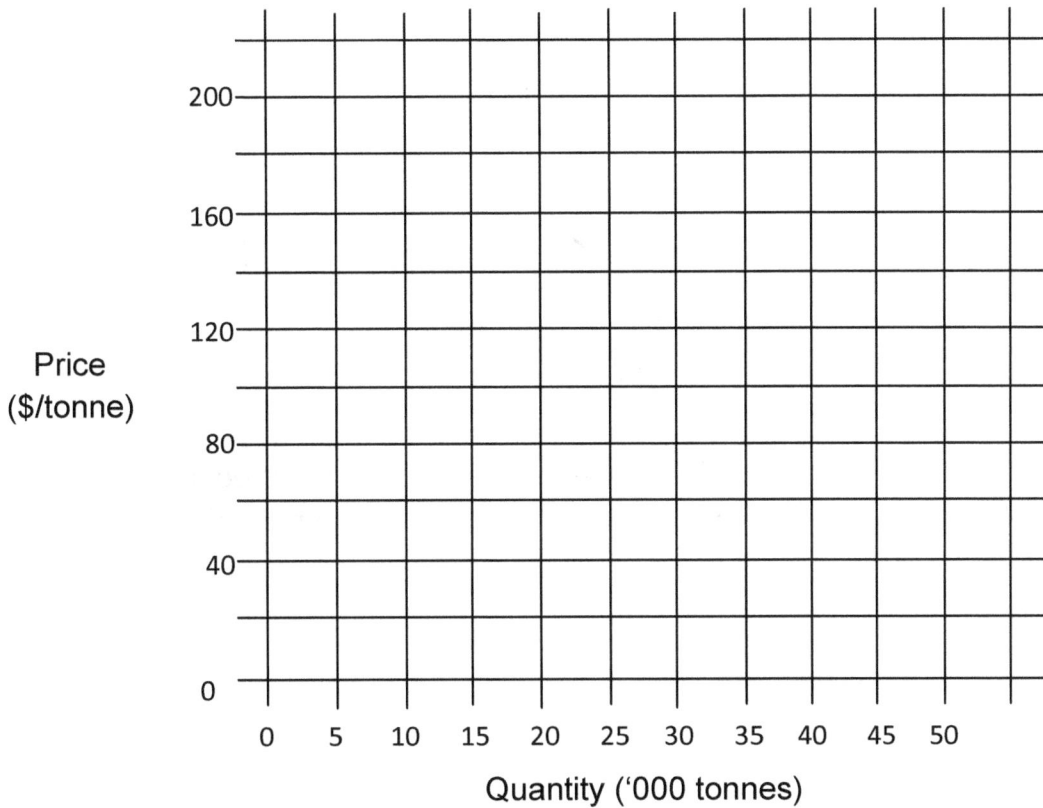

i) What would be the new equilibrium price and quantity after the imposition of the import quota?
[2m]

j) i) With the quota in place, how much steel would the German producers be able to sell? What is the new revenue of the foreign steel suppliers?   [3m]

ii) Why have the revenues of the foreign steel suppliers not been reduced as much as compared to the case when the tariff was implemented?   [2m]

2) The table below reflects the world price of iron ore and the production of iron ore by country X. Iron ore is the only export of this country and it exports all of its iron ore production.

Year	Price of Iron Ore ($ per tonne)	Index of Iron Ore Price	Iron Ore Production and Export (million tonnes)	Index of Iron Ore Production	Index of Import Prices
2005	110		6		90
2006	120		6.5		95
2007	140	100	7.2	100	100
2008	130		7.5		106
2009	180		6.2		110
2010	190		6.8		112

a) Taking 2007 as the base year, fill in the remaining columns for the table above.

[6m]

b) Find out the value of Country X's exports in 2005 and 2009.

[2m]

c) Calculate the Terms of Trade (ToT) for Country X from 2005 to 2010.   [5m]

d) Describe the trend in the ToT from 2005 to 2010.   [2m]

e) If the total import expenditure in 2005 was $530 million, calculate the value of Country X's net exports.   [2m]

f) If the balance of net exports calculated in part (e) is 30% of GDP, find the GDP for Country X.   [2m]

3) The table below shows the exchange rate for countries A and B, whose currencies are $ and € respectively.

Year	Exchange rate ($/€)
2010	1.75
2015	1.53

a) i) Which country's currency depreciated between 2010 and 2015?   [1m]

   ii) Find the depreciation of the currency as a percentage.   [2m]

b) If an IPhone 6 costs $1200 in 2015, how much would it cost in €?   [2m]

Experts have predicted the demand and supply functions for the € currency 20 years later to Qd = 10000 – 30000P and Qs = 2500 + 2000P, where P is the price of € in terms of $

c) What would then be the equilibrium exchange rate of € in terms of $?   [3m]

d) With the exchange rate obtained in part (c), what would be the exchange rate of $ in terms of €?   [2m]

e) Which currency was predicted to appreciate? By what percentage will it appreciate?   [2m]

4) Country A and B each produce 2 goods – cars and textiles.

At the moment, the resources of Country A can produce either 20 units of cars with no textiles or 80 units of textiles with no cars.

On the other hand, the resources of Country B can produce either 10 units of cars with no textiles or 50 units of textiles with no cars.

Assuming that both countries have the same resources, and if they were to devote all of their resources into producing cars, Country A will be able to produce 220 units of car while Country B will be able to produce 200 units of cars.

a) What is the opportunity cost of producing (i) 1 unit of car, and (ii) 1 unit of textile for both Countries A and B?   [4m]

b) Which country enjoys an absolute advantage in the production of (i) Cars, and (ii) Textiles?   [2m]

c) For which good does each country enjoy a comparative advantage over the other country?   [2m]

d) How do your answers in parts (a) and (c) help to determine whether the 2 countries should trade with each other? [3m]

e) Calculate the total number of cars and textiles that would be produced if both countries decide to specialise completely in accordance with the principle of comparative advantage. [4m]

f) If both countries wanted to be self-sufficient and did not trade, but devoted half of their resources to the production of cars and the other half to producing textiles, how much of each good could country A and B produce individually? [3m]

g) On the grid below, draw the production possibility graphs for country A and B with appropriate axes labelled. [4m]

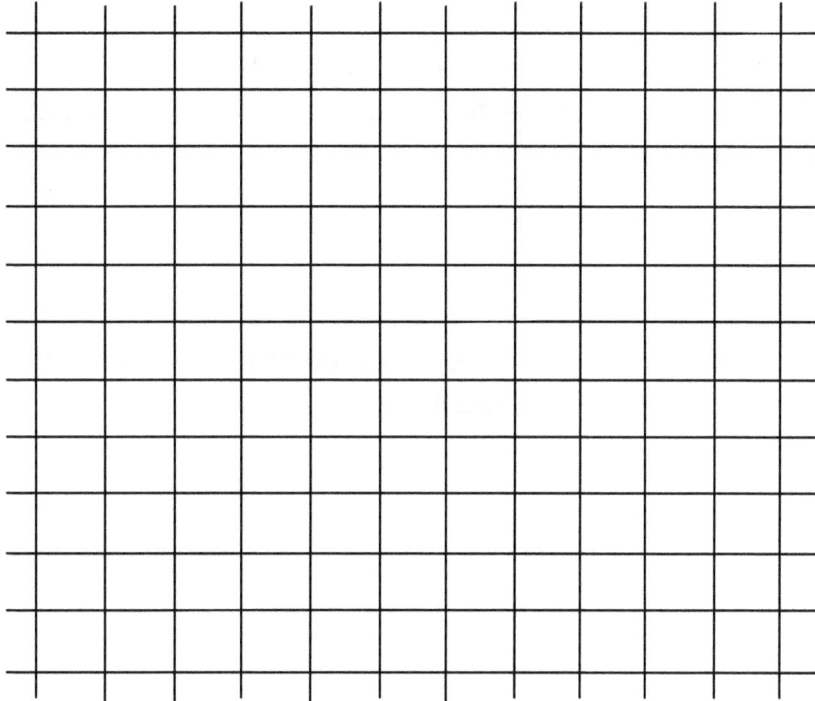

h) Assuming that Countries A and B specialise completely as in part (e), find an ideal terms of trade such that both countries would benefit and increase the total units of both their cars and textiles as compared to being self-sufficient as in part (f). [4m]

5) Country A operates under a fixed exchange rate currency regime. It is currently suffering from a balance of trade deficit of $1000 (import expenditure is $10000 and export revenue is $9000).

The government wishes to reduce the deficit through devaluing its currency by 20%. Economists estimate that the PED for the country's imports and exports are 0.6 and 0.3 respectively.

a) Will the devaluation of the currency have its intended effect? Explain your answer with reference to the data above. [6m]

b) Using calculations to support your answer, show that the devaluation would have a different effect if the PED of imports and exports were both 0.8. [4m]

6) Country B has just published its balance of payments accounts for 2014.

Exports of goods – $160 billion

Imports of goods – $100 billion

Exports of services – $4 billion

Imports of services – $30 billion

Income from foreign sources – $2 billion

Payments to foreign beneficiaries – $16 billion

Current transfers from foreign sources – $2 billion

Current transfers to foreign beneficiaries – $10 billion

Debt forgiveness and other capital transfers – $1 billion

Direct investment from foreign sources – $6 billion

Direct investment abroad from domestic sources – nil

Portfolio investment from foreign sources – nil

Portfolio investment abroad from domestic sources – $12 billion

Change in reserve assets – $7 billion

a) Calculate the following,

1) The balance of trade in goods. [2m]

2) The balance of trade in services, income and current transfers. [3m]

3) The overall current account balance. [2m]

4) The balance in the financial account. [2m]

A few months later, a large foreign multinational company was developed in country A and it began employing some expatriate technicians, as well as managers.

b) Which of the above entries in the accounts would likely be affected by the presence of the large multinational company? Explain your answer. [3m]

Answers and explanations to questions in Section 1

Question 1

a) Fill in the Qd and Qs columns in the following table.   [2m]

Price ($ per plate)	Qd (hundred plates)	Qs (hundred plates)
1	16	0
2	14	6
3	12	12
4	10	18
5	8	24

b) Plot and label the functions using the table of values calculated above.   [2m]

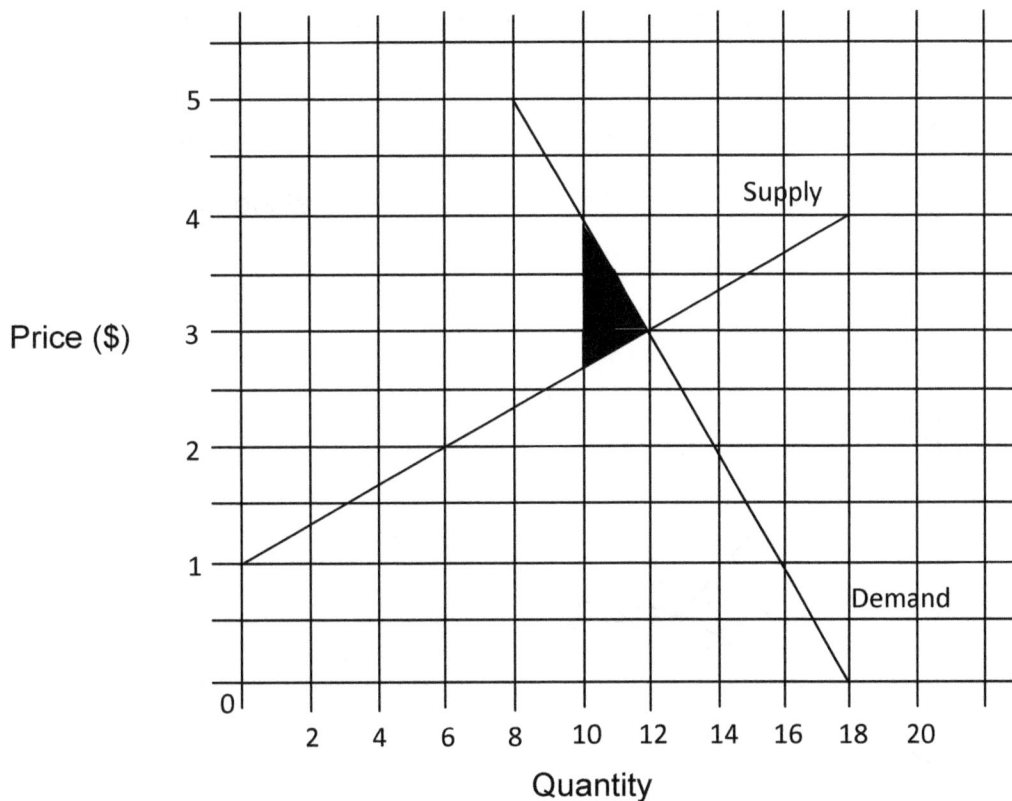

c) i) Calculate, using algebra, the equilibrium price and quantity implied by the intersection of the two functions. Check that it agrees with what is suggested by your graph from part (b). [2m]

Setting Qd = Qs and solving for P:

$$18 - 2P = -6 + 6P$$
$$24 = 8P$$
$$3 = P$$

Then substitute P = 3 in either (or both) equations and solve for Q:

Qd = 18 – 2P or	Qs = – 6 + 6P
Qd = 18 – 2(3)	Qs = – 6 + 6(3)
Qd = 12	Qs = 12

Confirming that at the equilibrium price $3, the Qd and Qs are both 12 as suggested by the graph.

ii) Find the consumer and producer surplus enjoyed at this equilibrium point. [2m]

When Qd = 0, 0 = 18 – 2P, P would be 9 as seen from the demand function.

Looking at the graph, we are looking at a welfare triangle that looks like:

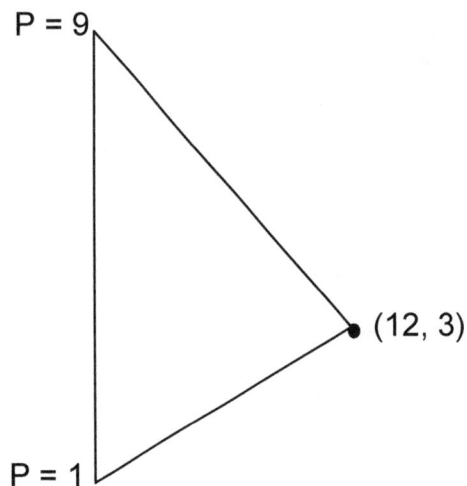

P = 9

(12, 3)

P = 1

Thus, the consumer surplus is the area represented by the following triangle:

P = 9

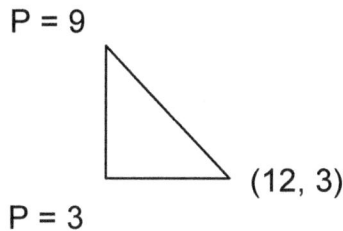

(12, 3)

P = 3

A = ½ Base x Height

A = ½ (12) (6)

A = 36, so the consumer surplus is $36

Meanwhile, the producer surplus is the area represented by the following triangle:

P = 3

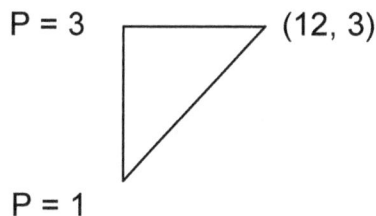

(12, 3)

P = 1

A = ½ Base x Height

A = ½ (12) (2)

A = 12, so the producer surplus is $12

d) i) Would there be a shortage or surplus in response and of how many units?

[2m]

If the government were to impose a price floor of $4,

$$Qd = 18 - 2P \qquad Qs = -6 + 6P$$
$$Qd = 18 - 2(4) \qquad Qs = -6 + 6(4)$$
$$Qd = 10 \qquad Qs = 18$$

Thus, as Qs is greater than Qd, there would be a surplus of 8 units.

ii) If the government decides to buy any quantity not sold in the market, what would be the total cost required?   [2m]

If the government decides to buy the surplus 8 units at the floor price, they would have to spend (8 units at $4 each) 8 x $4 = $32

e) Compare the producer revenue and consumer expenditure in this situation (the $4 price floor) with the producer revenue and consumer expenditure in the initial situation without the price floor.   [3m]

In the initial situation, producer revenue and consumer expenditure would both be (12 units at $3 each) 12 x $3 = $36.

However, after the price floor has been put into place, while suppliers want to sell 18 units, only 10 will actually change hands (quantity exchanged). Thus, producer revenue/consumer expenditure will increase to (10 units at $4 each) 10 x $4 = $40.

f) i) Calculate the producer and consumer surplus enjoyed at this point (after the $4 price floor)   [3m]

With a $4 price floor, the producer surplus can be represented by the irregular area above the supply curve from the vertical axis until Q = 10. I will decompose it into two regular shapes as follows:

A rectangle: P = 4 ⌐‾‾‾‾‾‾‾‾⌐ (10, 4)
                          | |
                 P = 2.67 ⌐_____⌐ (10, 2.67)

And a triangle: P = 2.67 ⌐‾‾‾‾‾‾‾⌐ (10, 2.67)
                          | ⟋
                 P = 1   ⌐⟋

The areas of each shape are: A = ½ Base x Height   and   A = Length x Width

A = ½ (10) (1.67)   A = 10 x 1.33
A = 8.35   A = 13.3

So the total producer surplus is 8.35 + 13.3 = $21.65

The consumer surplus is simpler to figure out, being just the area of the triangle below the demand curve from the vertical axis until Q = 10, as shown below:

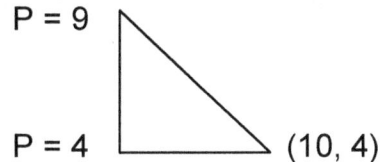

A = ½ Base x Height

A = ½ (10) (5)

A = 25 so the consumer surplus is $25

ii) Has the price floor transferred some surplus from consumers to producers and if so, how much?   [2m]

Yes. By looking at the results from part (cii), where the consumer surplus was $36 and the producer surplus was $12, we can see that some of the consumer surplus has been transferred to producers as a result of the price floor.

Welfare gained by producers = $21.65 – $12
                                            = $9.65

Thus, the price floor transferred $9.65 from consumers to producers.

iii) Has some welfare simply been lost? If so, shade the area of the welfare loss on the graph in (b) and calculate the extent of the welfare loss.   [3m]

Total welfare before price floor = $36 + $12
                                                = $48

Total welfare after price floor   = $25 + $21.65
                                                = $46.65

Yes, from the calculations, a welfare of ($48 – $46.65) = $1.35 has been lost.

Refer to graph for welfare loss shaded.

Answers and explanations to questions in Section 1

<u>Question 2</u>

    a) From the table of values, derive the demand and supply functions in the form of an equation $Q = A + BP$, where Q is the quantity of units, A and B are arbitrary constants while P is the price of each unit.   [4m]

For the demand function, taking $Qd = 60$, $P = 4.50$ and $Qd = 70$, $P = 4.00$,

We will have 2 simultaneous equations:

$$60 = A + B\,(4.5) \text{ and } 70 = A + B\,(4)$$

By solving these 2 equations, we will get $A = 150$ and $B = -20$

Thus, the demand function is $Qd = 150 - 20P$.

For the supply function, taking $Qs = 105$, $P = 4.50$ and $Qs = 100$, $P = 4.00$,

We will have 2 simultaneous equations:

$$105 = A + B\,(4.5) \text{ and } 100 = A + B\,(4)$$

By solving these 2 equations, we will get $A = 60$ and $B = 10$

Thus, the supply function is $Qs = 60 + 10P$.

b) Plot and label the demand and supply functions using the table of values above then identify the equilibrium price and quantity from the graph drawn.

[3m]

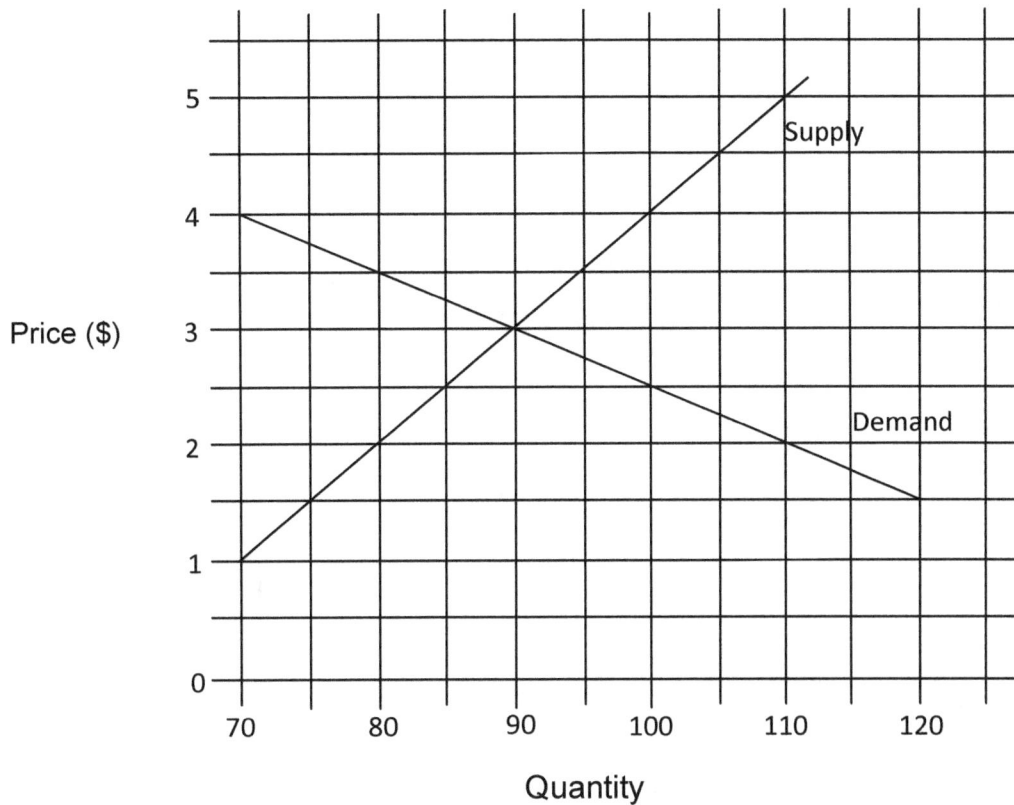

From the graph above, the equilibrium price and quantity is $3 at 90 units.

c) Calculate the price elasticity of demand for an increase in price from $3 per unit to $3.50 per unit.

[2m]

PED = % change in Qd ÷ % change in P

$\quad$ = − 10/90 ÷ 0.5/3

$\quad$ = − 0.667

d) From the two equations in (a),

i) How can you tell how many units consumers would want to buy at a price of zero? [1m]

Using the demand function Qd = 150 – 20P, I can easily see that at a price of zero, Qd = 150, as Qd = 150 – 20(0).

Hence, people would want to buy 150 units at a price of zero.

ii) At what price would the producers supply the quantity of goods as calculated in d) i)? [2m]

Using the supply function, set Qs = 150 and solve for P,

$$150 = 60 + 10P$$
$$90 = 10P$$
$$9 = P$$

Hence, the producers would supply 150 units at a price of $9.

e) If the demand for good Y becomes relatively more price elastic in the long run, what would happen to the quantity demanded when its price increases? [2m]

As the demand for good Y becomes more price elastic, the quantity demanded will become more responsive to changes in price. Hence, when its price increases, the quantity demanded will decrease more than proportionately to the increase in prices.

f) Would a decrease in the price of good X cause an increase or decrease in the demand of good Y. Why? [2m]

A decrease in the price of good X would cause a decrease in the demand for good Y. As both goods X and Y are substitutes, a cheaper good X will lead to consumers switching from Y to X. This means the demand for good Y is falling as the quantity demanded for X increases.

g) State the equation for the new demand function. [2m]

Since Qd has decreased by 30 units at all prices, the new equation will be

$$Qd = (150 - 30) - 20P$$

$$= 120 - 20P$$

h) Find the new equilibrium price and quantity. [2m]

Setting Qd = Qs and solving for P:

$$120 - 20P = 60 + 10P$$

$$60 = 30P$$

$$2 = P$$

Then substitute P = 2 in either (or both) equations and solve for Q:

Qd = 120 – 20P	Qs = 60 + 10P
Qd = 120 – 20(2)	Qs = 60 + 10(2)
Qd = 80	Qs = 80

Hence, the new equilibrium price and quantity is $2 and 80 units.

<u>Question 3</u>

a) Calculate the consumer and producer surplus from the diagram above.   [2m]

Looking at the graph, the consumer surplus is the area represented by the following triangle:

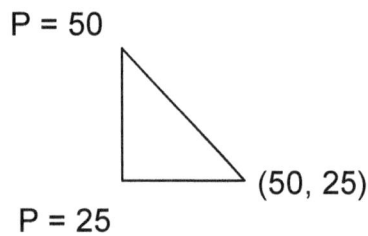

P = 50

P = 25   (50, 25)

A = ½ Base x Height

A = ½ (25) (50)

A = 625, so the consumer surplus is $625

Meanwhile, the producer surplus is the area represented by the following triangle:

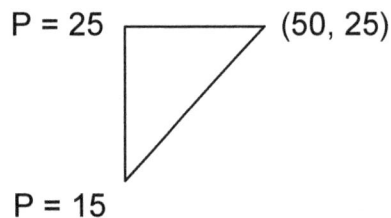

P = 25   (50, 25)

P = 15

A = ½ Base x Height

A = ½ (10) (50)

A = 250, so the producer surplus is $250

b) Copy the above diagram and apply a specific indirect tax of $5 per unit to the handbags. Plot the resultant supply and demand curves on the same diagram.

[2m]

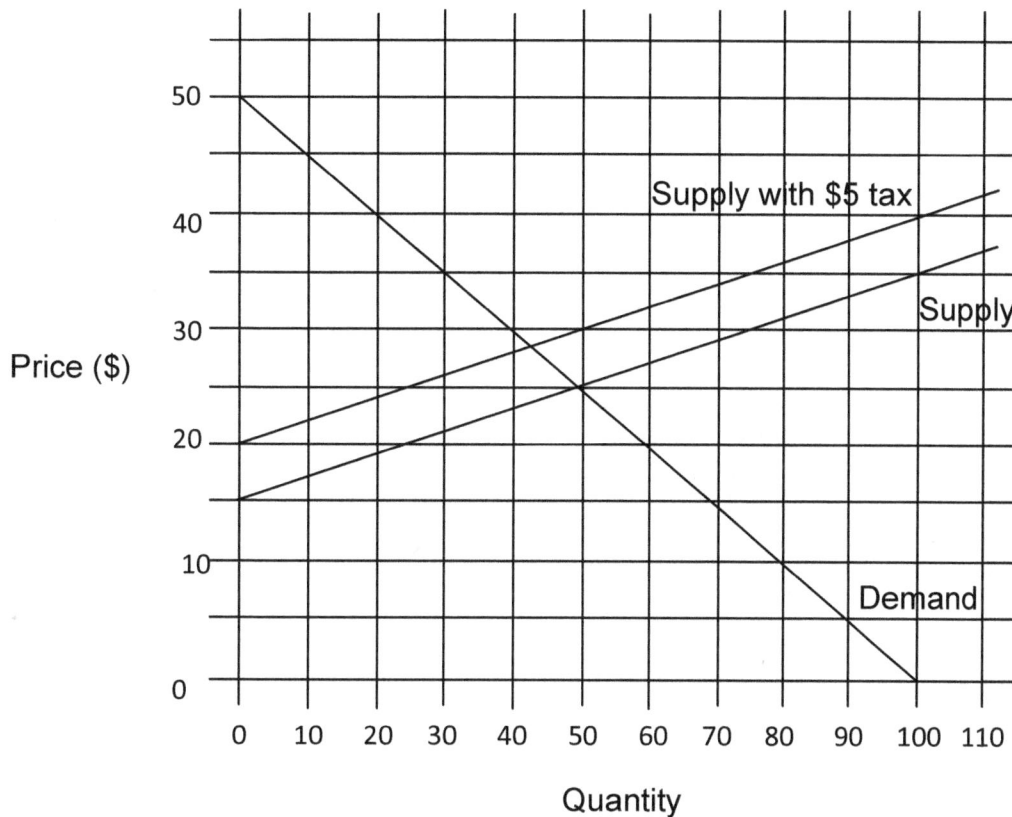

c) Using the graph drawn in (b), determine the new equilibrium price and quantity. Hence, calculate the total tax revenue to the government. [5m]

From the graph, the original supply function can be obtained by:

Taking Qs = 50, P = 25 and Qs = 0, P = 15,

We will have 2 simultaneous equations:

50 = A + B (25) and 0 = A + B (15)

By solving these 2 equations, we will get A = − 75 and B = 5

Thus, the supply function is Qs = − 75 + 5P.

Hence, the new supply function will be Qs = − 75 + 5 (P − 5)

$$= -75 + 5P - 25$$

$$= -100 + 5P$$

The demand function can be obtained by:

Taking Qd = 50, P = 25 and Qd = 0, P = 50,

We will have 2 simultaneous equations:

50 = A + B (25) and 0 = A + B (50)

By solving these 2 equations, we will get A = 100 and B = − 2

Thus, the demand function is Qd = 100 − 2P.

Setting Qd = Qs and solving for P:

$$100 - 2P = -100 + 5P$$

$$200 = 7P$$

$$28.6 = P$$

Then substitute P = 28.6 in either (or both) equations and solve for Q:

Qd = 100 − 2P or Qs = − 100 + 5P

Qd = 100 − 2 (28.6) Qs = − 100 + 5 (28.6)

Qd = 43 Qs = 43 (nearest whole number)

Thus, the new equilibrium price and quantity is $28.60 and 43 units.

Hence, the total tax revenue to the government is 43 x $5 = $215.

d) Calculate the new consumer and producer surplus after the tax has been implemented. [2m]

Looking at the graph, the consumer surplus is the area represented by the following triangle:

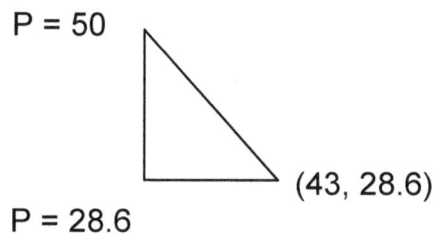

P = 50

P = 28.6

(43, 28.6)

A = ½ Base x Height

A = ½ (43) (21.4)

A = 460.1, so the consumer surplus is $460.10

Meanwhile, the producer surplus is the area represented by the following triangle:

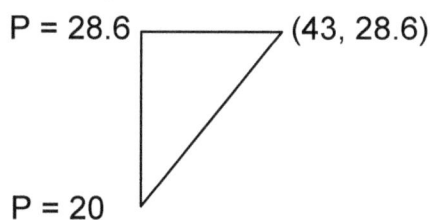

P = 28.6

(43, 28.6)

P = 20

A = ½ Base x Height

A = ½ (43) (8.6)

A = 184.9, so the producer surplus is $184.90

e) By considering the sum of the post-tax consumer and producer surplus and the tax revenue to the government, as well as the sum of the consumer and producer surplus before the tax was implemented, what has been the impact of the tax on the overall welfare? [3m]

Sum of the post-tax consumer and producer surplus and the tax revenue

$$= \$460.10 + \$184.90 + \$215$$

$$= \$860$$

Sum of the consumer and producer surplus before the tax

$$= \$625 + \$250$$

$$= \$875$$

Thus, we can conclude that the tax has led to a decrease in overall welfare of $875 – $860 = $15

Question 4

a) Calculate the consumer expenditure and producer revenue from the diagram.

[2m]

From the diagram, the consumer expenditure and producer revenue are equal and can be represented by the following rectangle:

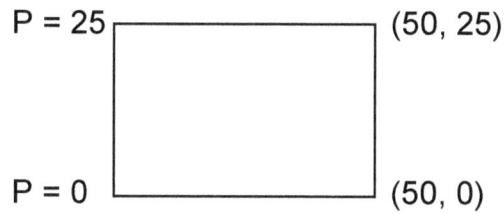

P = 25 ┌──────────┐ (50, 25)
       │   │
       │   │
       │   │
P = 0 └──────────┘ (50, 0)

A = Length x Breadth

A = 25 x 50

A = 1250

Hence, the consumer expenditure, and producer revenue are both $1250.

b) Copy the diagram and apply a specific indirect subsidy of $5 per unit to the handbags. Plot the resultant supply and demand curves on the same diagram.

[2m]

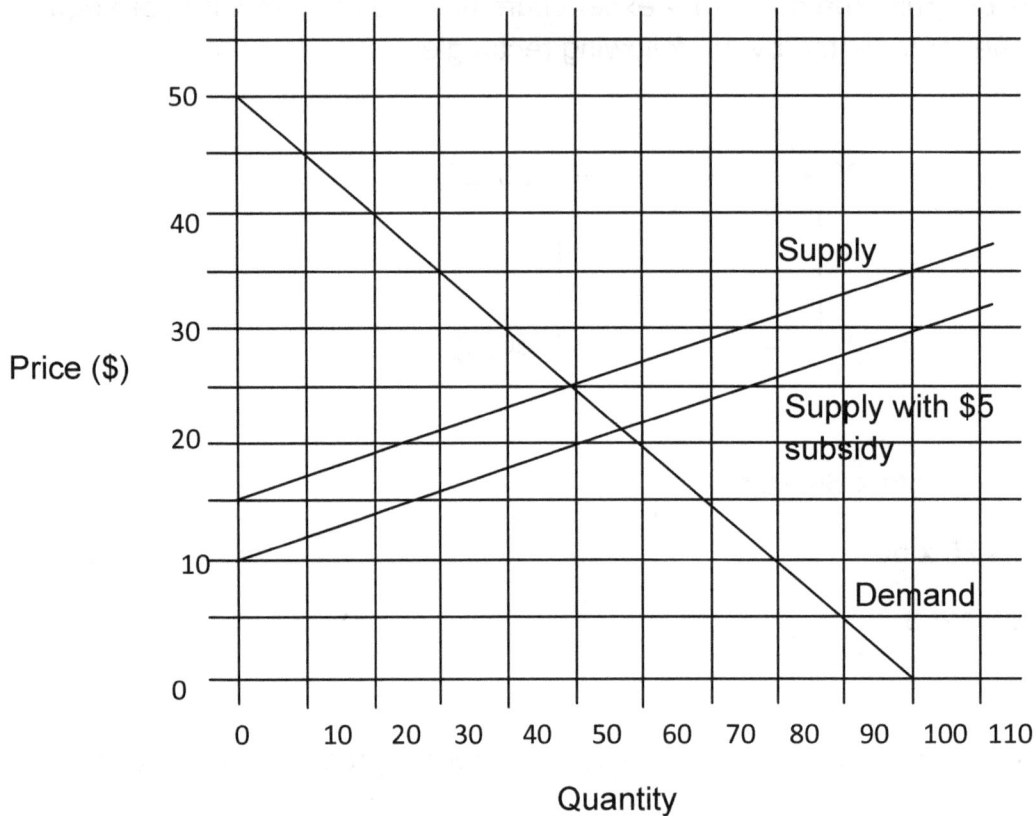

c) Determine the new equilibrium price and quantity. [3m]

From (3c), the supply function is Qs = − 75 + 5P.

Hence, the new 'Supply with $5 subsidy' function will be

$$Qs = -75 + 5(P + 5)$$

$$= -75 + 5P + 25$$

$$= -50 + 5P$$

Similarly from (3c), the demand function is Qd = 100 − 2P.

Setting Qd = Qs and solving for P:

$$100 - 2P = -50 + 5P$$

$$150 = 7P$$

$$21.4 = P$$

Then substitute P = 21.4 in either (or both) equations and solve for Q:

Qd = 100 – 2P or	Qs = – 50 + 5P
Qd = 100 – 2 (21.4)	Qs = – 50 + 5 (21.4)
Qd = 57	Qs = 57(nearest whole number)

Thus, the new equilibrium price and quantity is $21.40 and 57 units.

d) i) Calculate the consumer expenditure and producer revenue after the subsidy was applied.   [2m]

After the subsidy was granted, consumers spent:

$$57 \times \$21.40 = \$1219.80$$

While producers would have received:

$$57 \times \$26.40 = \$1504.80$$

ii) After making necessary comparisons on both the consumer expenditure and producer revenue before and after the subsidy, determine the impact of the subsidy on each.   [2m]

Comparing $1219.80 and $1504.80 to the initial consumer expenditure/ producer revenue of $1250, we can see that the subsidy has resulted in a slight reduction in consumer expenditure and a significant increase in producer revenue.

e) i) Calculate the incidence of the subsidy on both the consumer and producer.

[3m]

Comparing the initial equilibrium price of $25 with the post-subsidy equilibrium price of $21.40, we can see that $3.60 of the $5 subsidy has been transferred to consumers, whereas producers are only gaining $1.40.

Hence, the incidence on the consumers = $3.60 x 57

$$= \$205.20$$

While the incidence on the producers = $1.40 x 57

$$= \$79.80$$

ii) Who benefited more from the subsidy? Explain why this is so.   [2m]

The consumers are enjoying a greater portion of the subsidy than the producers. This is because the demand for handbags is relatively price inelastic (PED<1) and when faced with a subsidy, the increase in quantity demanded would be less than proportionate to the decrease in price. Thus, to clear the surplus that has arisen from the increase in supply, a greater fall in prices would be required to get the consumers to purchase more.

This being the case, the subsidy in this instance lowers consumer prices more than it increases producer prices (inclusive of subsidy) and thus, a larger portion of the benefit goes to the consumers.

Answers and explanations to questions in Section 2

Question 1

a) Copy the table above and,

    i) Calculate the marginal output of each additional harvester.   [2m]

    ii) Calculate the average output attributable to each harvester for all quantities of harvesters.   [2m]

Number of harvesters	Output of papayas (tonnes)	Marginal Output (tonnes)	Average Output (tonnes)
0	10	-	-
1	25	15	25
2	46	21	23
3	69	23	23
4	88	19	22
5	100	12	20
6	108	8	18
7	112	4	16
8	112	0	14

b) At what point does the farmer begin suffering diminishing returns from using additional harvesters? [2m]

Since the marginal output for the 3rd harvester is 23 and the marginal output for the 4th harvester is 19, the farmer began suffering diminishing returns from using the 4th harvester.

c) Calculate the total cost of producing 100 tonnes of papayas. [2m]

From the table, producing 100 tonnes of papayas would require 5 harvesters.

Hence, 5 x $6000

= $30000

d) Calculate the value of papayas produced by the 6th harvester. [2m]

From the table, the 6th harvester produces an additional 8 tonnes of papayas.

Thus, the value = 8 x $500
= $4000

e) i) How many harvesters should the farmer use to maximise his returns? Explain your answer. [3m]

The farmer should use 5 harvesters to maximise his returns.

The marginal revenue from his 5th harvester is 12 x $500/tonne = $6000.

The marginal cost of the 5th harvester is also $6000.

If the farmer were to maximise his returns, he would employ harvesters up to a point where the marginal revenue is equal the marginal cost of employing another harvester.

ii) What would be the total profit if the farmer decides to employ that number of harvesters as calculated above in part e) i)? [2m]

Total profit = Total Revenue – Total Cost
= (100 x $500) – (5 x $6000)
= $50000 – $30000
= $20000

f) How would this affect his profit maximising output? [1m]

A tax on profit would have no effect on the profit maximizing output because it does not affect the value of the marginal revenue or the marginal cost. Hence, the marginal revenue still equals to the marginal cost when 100 units of papayas are produced.

g) Calculate the new level of profit as well as the government revenue from the tax. [3m]

The new level of profit will be 85% of the original profit after the tax.

New level of profit = 85% x $20000
= $17000

Thus, government revenue = $20000 – $17000
= $3000

<u>Question 2</u>

a) From the table above, what are the store's fixed costs? Explain your answer.

[2m]

The store's fixed costs are $20, as these are its costs when output is equal to zero, indicating that these costs do not vary according to output.

b) Thus, calculate the average variable cost where output is 5 units.   [2m]

Total cost where output is 5 units = $50

Total variable costs = $50 − $20
           = $30

Hence, average variable costs where output is 5 units = $30 ÷ 5
                    = $6

Answers and explanations to questions in Section 2

c) Copy the table above and,

    i) Calculate the store's marginal and average cost,   [2m]

    ii) As well as marginal and average revenue, at each level of output.   [2m]

Output	Total Costs ($)	Marginal Costs ($)	Average costs ($)	Total Revenue ($)	Marginal Revenue ($)	Average Revenue ($)
0	20	–	–	0	–	–
1	30	10	30	24	24	24
2	38	8	19	44	20	22
3	44	6	14.6	60	16	20
4	48	4	12	72	12	18
5	50	2	10	80	8	16
6	54	4	9	84	4	14
7	60	6	8.6	84	0	12
8	68	8	8.5	80	– 4	10
9	78	10	8.6	72	– 8	8
10	90	12	9	60	– 12	6

d) i) Find the average fixed costs,   [2m]

Average fixed costs = Total fixed costs ÷ Output

= $20 ÷ 4 = $5

ii) And the average variable costs.   [2m]

Average variable costs = Total variable costs ÷ Output

= (Total costs – Total fixed costs) ÷ Output

= ($48 – $20) ÷ 4

= $24 ÷ 4

= $6

e) i) Calculate the store's profit maximising output.   [4m]

The profit maximising output occurs where Marginal Cost = Marginal revenue. From the table above, we can see that at output = 6 units, both the MC and MR are $4.

Whereas at output = 5 units, MR exceeds MC and thus more profit could still be made if output was increased. And at output = 7 units, MC exceeds MR and thus more profit could be made by producing less.

Hence, the store's profit maximising output is 6 units.

ii) Find the total profit at that point and determine the type of profit.   [3m]

Total profit = Total Revenue – Total Cost
= $84 – $54
= $30

Since total revenue exceeds total costs, the store is making supernormal profits.

f) What would be the store's revenue-maximizing output? [2m]

From the table above, the store's revenue-maximizing output occurs when output = 6 or 7 units, where the total revenue is the highest at $84.

g) What would you expect to happen in this market in the long run and how would it affect the store's pricing and output decisions. [2m]

In the long run, new firms will be attracted by the supernormal profits of the store and enter this market. With the increase in the supply of goods, prices would then gradually fall, resulting in each firm producing lesser and lesser until a normal profit is achieved in the market.

h) i) On the grid below, plot the store's marginal and average costs curves as well as marginal and average revenue curves. [4m]

ii) On the graphs plotted, mark in the profit maximising and revenue maximising points as A and B respectively. [2m]

Costs/ Revenue ($)

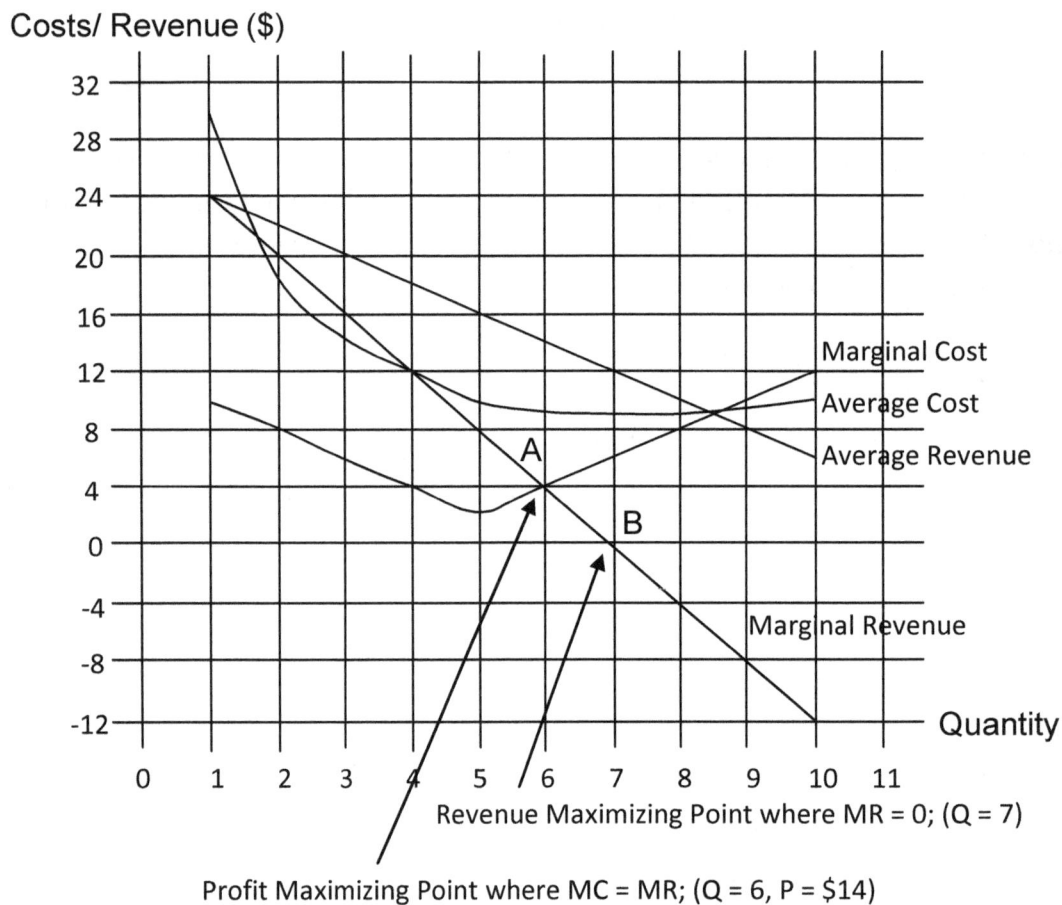

Revenue Maximizing Point where MR = 0; (Q = 7)

Profit Maximizing Point where MC = MR; (Q = 6, P = $14)

Answers and explanations to questions in Section 2

Question 3

a) Copy and complete the table above after calculating the relevant costs and revenues. [5m]

Quantity of cookies	Total costs($)	Variable costs($)	Marginal costs($)	Average variable costs($)	Average total costs($)	Total revenue ($)	Marginal revenue ($)
0	0.5	–	–	–	–	0	–
1	3	2.5	2.5	2.5	3	5	5
2	4.5	4	1.5	2	2.25	9.5	4.5
3	6.5	6	2	2	2.16	13.5	4
4	9	8.5	2.5	2.13	2.25	17	3.5
5	12	11.5	3	2.3	2.4	20	3
6	15.5	15	3.5	2.5	2.58	22.5	2.5
7	19.5	19	4	2.71	2.79	24.5	2
8	24	23.5	4.5	2.94	3	26	1.5

Answers and explanations to questions in Section 2

b) i) At what price would each cookie be sold at if 5 cookies were produced?

[2m]

At output = 5 units, total revenue = $20

Price = Total revenue ÷ Quantity

$$= \$20 \div 5$$

$$= \$4$$

ii) What is the profit from each cookie?

[2m]

Total profit = Total Revenue − Total Cost

$$= \$20 - \$12$$

$$= \$8$$

Profit from each cookie = $8 ÷ 5

$$= \$1.60$$

c) Determine the profit maximising output and price for the cookie manufacturer.

[4m]

The profit maximising output occurs where Marginal Cost = Marginal revenue. From the table above, we can see that at output = 5 units, both the MC and MR are $3.

Whereas at output = 4 units, MR exceeds MC and thus more profit could still be made if output was increased. And at output = 6 units, MC exceeds MR and thus more profits could be earned by reducing output.

d) If the fixed costs for the cookie manufacturer were to double, how would the profit maximizing price and quantity be affected? Why?

[2m]

If the fixed costs for the cookie manufacturer were to double, the profit maximizing price and quantity will be unaffected as both the MC and MR are unaffected.

e) Is this pie seller operating in a perfectly competitive market? Explain your answer.
[2m]

The pie seller is not operating in a perfectly competitive market because it faces a downward sloping demand and not a perfectly elastic demand as seen from the decreasing marginal revenue values from the table.

f) i) At which level of output are average variable costs at a minimum? [1m]

From the table, average variable costs are at a minimum of $2 when output = 2 or 3 units.

ii) What is likely to happen if the selling price of the manufacturer's cookie is below this minimum amount? [2m]

If the selling price of the pies is below $2, the pie seller is likely to shut down as every unit produced will result in additional losses to him.

iii) What is likely to happen if the selling price of the manufacturer's cookie is above the minimum average variable cost but below the minimum average total cost? [2m]

If the selling price of the pies is between $2 and $2.16, the pie seller will likely stay in business but operate at a loss.

This is because, since the pie seller would have to pay for the fixed costs regardless of the output level, shutting down and not obtaining any revenue will result in his losses to be even greater.

For instance, if the price of pies were $2.10, and if the pie seller were to sell 3 pies, he would earn $6.30. This suggests a loss of $0.20 as the total cost to produce 3 pies is $6.50. This loss of $0.20 is less than the loss that would be incurred if the pie seller were to shut down and still be responsible for the fixed costs of $0.50.

g) If the market price for cookies increased to $4, calculate the new profit maximising output and new level of profit. [4m]

If the market price for cookies increased to $4, the new profit maximising output would increase to 7 units where MC = MR = $4.

New level of profit = Total Revenue – Total Cost

$$= \$24.50 - \$19.50$$

$$= \$5$$

h) Calculate the PED necessary for a price change to increase the quantity of cookies sold from 4 to 6. [4m]

The price change necessary for an increase in quantity of cookies sold from 4 to 6 is from $4.25 to $3.75.

$$PED = \frac{\% \ change \ in \ Quantity \ Demanded}{\% \ change \ in \ Price}$$

$$= \frac{50\%}{11.8\%}$$

$$= 4.25$$

Answers and explanations to questions in Section 2

Question 4

a) Complete the table above after calculating the relevant quantities and revenues.

[4m]

Price ($)	20	18	16	14	12	10	8	6	4
Qd	0	1	2	3	4	5	6	7	8
Total Revenue ($)	0	18	32	42	48	50	48	42	32
Marginal Revenue ($)	–	18	14	10	6	2	– 2	– 6	– 10
Average revenue ($)	–	18	16	14	12	10	8	6	4

Answers and explanations to questions in Section 2

b) i) On the grid below, plot the monopolist's marginal cost curve, along with the marginal and average revenue curves. [3m]

ii) Identify the point on the graph which is allocative efficient and label the point, A. Explain your answer. [2m]

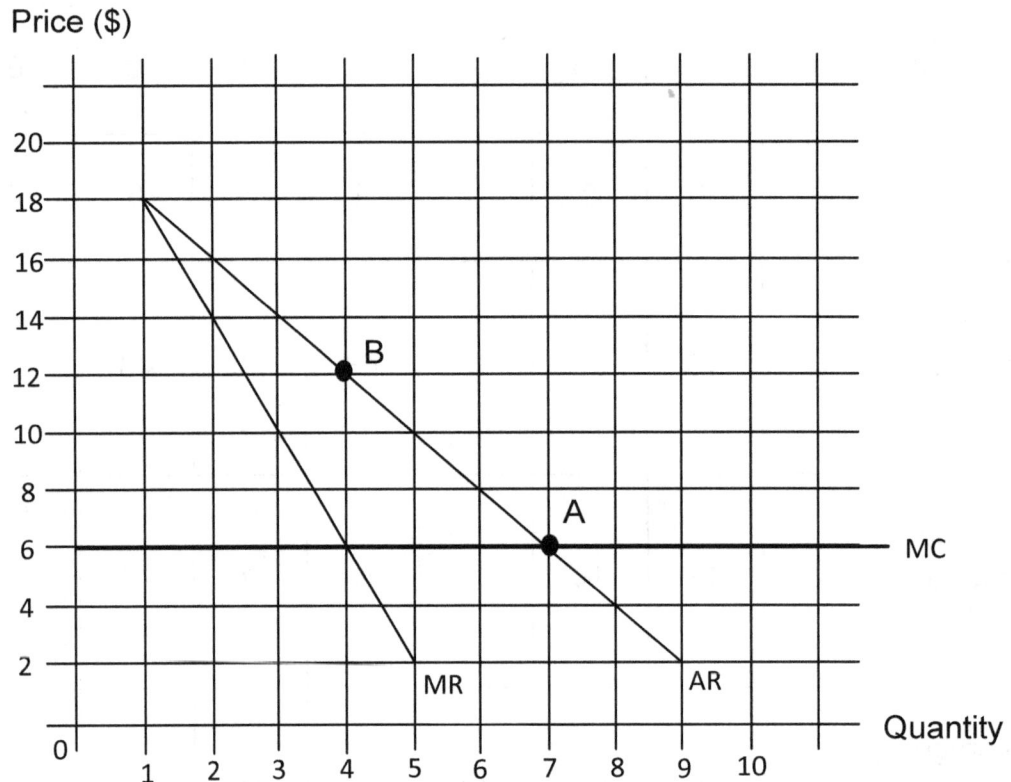

Allocative efficiency is achieved when production is at P = MC = $6.
7 units is therefore the allocatively efficient amount of output that maximises societal welfare.

iii) How would the allocatively efficient price in (bii) affect the monopolist's profitability? [2m]

Since MC is fixed, AVC is therefore also equal to the MC, which is $6. With the allocatively efficient price of $6, the total variable costs would be equal to the total revenue and so there would be an economic loss of the amount of fixed costs of $10.

c) i) Calculate the profit maximising output and price for the monopolist, as well as the maximum profit.   [5m]

The profit maximising output occurs where Marginal Cost = Marginal revenue. From the graph above, we can see that at output = 4 units, both the MC and MR are $6.

Whereas at output = 3 units, MR = $10 exceeds MC = $6 and thus more profit could still be made if output was increased. And at output = 5 units, MC = $6 exceeds MR = $2 and thus losses are incurred while producing an additional unit. Higher profit could be earned by reducing output.

Maximum profit = Total revenue – Total Variable costs – Total fixed costs

$$= (\$12 \times 4) - (\$6 \times 4) - \$10$$

$$= \$48 - \$24 - \$10$$

$$= \$14$$

ii) Label the profit maximising point on the graph drawn in (b) as B.   [2m]

Refer to the graph above.

d) From the graph, calculate the producer and consumer surplus,

i) At the allocative efficient point, A.   [2m]

There is no producer surplus as all output is priced equal to the marginal cost.

Consumer surplus is the area of the triangle from $6 to $20 and from output 0 to output 7, calculated as:

$$A = \tfrac{1}{2} \times \text{Base} \times \text{Height}$$

$$A = \tfrac{1}{2} \times (14) \times 7$$

$$A = 49$$

Hence, the consumer surplus is $49.

ii) At the profit maximising point, B. [2m]

The producer surplus would be the rectangle from output 0 to 4 and from price $6 to $12, calculated as:

$$A = 4 \times 6$$

$$A = 24, \text{ so the producer surplus is } \$24.$$

Consumer surplus can be calculated by taking the area of the triangle from output 0 to 4 and between the price $12 and $20, as follows:

$$A = \tfrac{1}{2} \times \text{Base} \times \text{Height}$$

$$A = \tfrac{1}{2} \times 4 \times 8$$

$$A = 16, \text{ so the consumer surplus is } \$16.$$

Hence, the consumer surplus is $16 while the producer surplus is $24.

iii) How much surplus was transferred from consumers to the monopolist, and how much became the deadweight loss. [3m]

$24 of surplus was transferred from consumers to producers and, as initially consumer surplus was $49, clearly $9 was simply lost. We can confirm this loss by calculating the area of the welfare loss triangle, which is the triangle beneath the AR curve between output 4 and 7 from $6 to $12 as follows:

$$A = \tfrac{1}{2} \times \text{Base} \times \text{Height}$$

$$A = \tfrac{1}{2} \times 3 \times 6$$

$$A = 9$$

Hence, $24 was transferred from consumers to producers while the welfare loss is $9.

Answers and explanations to questions in Section 2

e) Calculate the new producer and consumer surplus after the tax and calculate the new extent of the welfare loss to determine whether or not the tax would achieve the government's aim. [4m]

If the government implements a specific indirect tax of $4 for every unit of the product, the new profit maximising price and quantity would be $10 and 3 units.

So, taking this new equilibrium point, we can see that the consumer surplus is now represented by the triangle from Q = 0 to Q = 3 and from P = $14 to P = $20, which can be calculated as follows:

A = ½ x Base x Height
A = ½ x 3 x 6
A = 9, so the consumer surplus is now $9

Producer surplus is represented by the area of the rectangle from Q = 0 to Q = 3 between P = $10 and P = $14, and can be calculated as follows:

A = 3 x 4, so the producer surplus is now $12

The tax revenue for the government is represented by the area of the rectangle from Q = 0 to Q = 3 between P = $6 and P = $10, which can be calculated as follows:

A = 3 x 4, so the tax revenue is $12

Thus, total welfare is now $9 + $12 + $12 = $33, suggesting that the welfare loss has actually increased from $9 previously, to $16 due to the tax.

Hence, the tax did not achieve the government's aim but instead, worsen the situation of welfare loss.

f) If the marginal cost becomes zero, what would be the new profit maximising price?

[2m]

Profit maximising equilibrium occurs where MR=MC=0. This occurs when output is 5.5 units. Therefore the new profit maximising output is 5 units (since it does not make sense for producers to produce 0.5 unit). Based on 5 units produced, the new profit maximising price will be $10.

Answers and explanations to questions in Part 2

Question 1

a) Calculate the Gross Domestic Product (GDP) of country Y.   [2m]

GDP = Total Spending

$\quad$ = C + I + G+ (X – M)

$\quad$ = \$45bn + \$12.5bn + \$20bn + (\$7.5bn – \$10bn)

$\quad$ = \$75bn

b) Find out the Net National Product (NNP) of country Y. How would it be different from that of the GDP value?   [4m]

NNP = [GDP – Capital Consumption] + net property income from abroad
$\quad\quad\quad$ (for finding of NET value) $\quad\quad\quad\quad\quad\quad$ (for finding national product)

$\quad$ = [\$75bn - \$5bn] + (– \$2.5bn)

$\quad$ = \$67.5bn

GDP refers to the domestic value of all goods and services produced within the domestic territory of the nation, irrespective of differentiation between earnings by citizens or non-citizens.

GNP refers to the value of goods and services produced by the citizens in the geographical boundary of their country as well as all around the world subtracted by the property income to abroad.

Net National Product takes into account the depreciation of capital goods and therefore the value of capital consumption is deducted.

Given that the net property income from abroad is negative, which means that there is net outflow of income, the NNP is lower than the GDP value.

c) What is the total value of injections into Country Y?   [2m]

Injections = I + G + X

$\quad$ = \$12.5bn +\$20bn + \$7.5bn

$\quad$ = \$40bn

d) Calculate the total value of withdrawals in order for the income of the country to be in equilibrium. [2m]

In order for the income of the country to be in equilibrium, the total value of injections needs to be equal to the total value of withdrawals.

Injections = Withdrawals

= $40bn

e) Calculate the external deficit as a percentage of GDP for country Y. [2m]

Percentage = $2.5bn/$75bn

= 3.33%

Note: Question already specifies deficit. Hence $2.5bn is the size of the deficit. If question requires the Balance of Trade, then it is correct to answer -$2.5bn, which indicates a deficit.

f) Find out the value of the multiplier. [2m]

The value of the multiplier = 1/ (1 – MPC)

= 1/MPW

= 1/0.5

= 2

g) Calculate the new equilibrium level of income. [2m]

An increase in G from $20bn to $25bn is an increase of $5bn.

New equilibrium level of income = Original income + the change in income through the multiplier

= $75bn + ($5bn x 2)

= $85bn

h) What would be the new value of Consumption? [2m]

New value of Consumption = Original value + (Increase in income x MPC)

= $45bn + (0.5 x $10bn)

= $50bn

i) Calculate the new value of Imports. [2m]

New value of Imports = Original value + (Increase in income x MPM)

= $10bn + (0.2 x $10bn)

= $12bn

Answers and explanations to questions in Part 2

<u>Question 2</u>

a) Complete the table above by filling in the S column.   [2m]

Y ($million)	C ($million)	S ($million)	I ($million)
0	100	- 100	20
50	130	- 80	20
100	160	- 60	20
150	190	- 40	20
200	220	- 20	20
250	250	0	20
300	280	20	20
350	310	40	20
400	340	60	20
450	370	80	20
500	400	100	20

Answers and explanations to questions in Part 2

b) Find the equilibrium level of income. [2m]

Equilibrium income is established where Y = C + I. This occurs at Y = 300.

Thus, the equilibrium level of income would be $300million.

c) Calculate the value of MPC and MPS for this economy. [2m]

MPC = Change in C/ Change in Y

    = 30/50

    = 0.6

MPS = 1 - MPC

    = 1 - 0.6

    = 0.4

d) At what level of income is the Average Propensity to Consume = 1. [2m]

Average Propensity to Consume (APC) = C/Y

In order for APC to be equals to 1, C will be equal to Y.

From the table above, this occurs at C = Y= $250 million.

e) Calculate the value of the multiplier [2m]

The value of the multiplier is 1/MPS = 1/0.4

    = 2.5

f) Find the new equilibrium level of income.   [2m]

The new equilibrium level of income will be where (C+I) = Y.

If I increases to 80, C + 80 = Y occurs at Y = 450.

Thus the new equilibrium level of income is $450million.

g) If full employment is at Y = 500, calculate the size of the deflationary gap. [2m]

The deflationary gap = Yf – (C+I).
If full employment occurs at Y = 500, 500 - 450

$$= 50$$

Thus, the size of the deflationary gap is 500 - 450

$$= \$50million.$$

h) Determine the increase in investment level necessary to close the deflationary gap calculated in (g).   [2m]

The change in I need to close the gap = (Change in Y)/multiplier

$$= 50/2.5$$

$$= 20$$

Answers and explanations to questions in Part 2

Question 3

a) Calculate the nominal GDP in country X in 2005 and 2010.   [2m]

Nominal GDP = Value of output

= Output X Price

Nominal GDP in 2005 = ($100 X 2) + ($100 X 3) + ($100 X 1)

= $600

Nominal GDP in 2010 = ($200 X 3) + ($250 X 4) + ($140 X 1.5)

= $1810

b) What was the nominal rate of economic growth between 2005 and 2010?

[2m]

Nominal rate of economic growth = ($1810 – $600)/$600 X 100%

= 201.6%

c) Find out the real GDP in 2010 at 2005 prices.   [4m]

To find real GDP for 2010 at 2005 prices, multiply 2010 output by 2005 prices.

Toiletries = $200 X 2 = $400

Utensils = $250 X 3 = $750

Stationaries = $140 X 1 = $140

Thus, real GDP in 2010 = $400 + $750 + $140
= $1290

Answers and explanations to questions in Part 2

d) Calculate the percentage increase in real GDP from 2005 to 2010. [2m]

Percentage increase in real GDP from 2005 to 2010

= ($1290 − $600)/$600 X 100%

= 115%

e) Explain the difference between the real and nominal GDP growth from 2005 to 2010 for country X. [3m]

The nominal GDP growth did not take into account of the inflation that occurred since 2005 and thus reflected a higher growth than actual. For the real GDP growth, it measures the increase in output levels for the different goods while keeping their prices constant. That removes the effects of inflation, reflecting a more accurate growth rate.

f) Calculate the nominal GDP from the expenditure side for 2015. [2m]

Nominal GDP = C + I + G + (X − M)

= 100 + 15 + 20 + (31 − 30)

= $136 billion

g) If country X has a national population of 17 million, what would be its nominal GDP per capita? [2m]

Nominal GDP per capita = $136 billion / 17 million

= $8000

h) If the country's GDP deflator was set at '100' in 2014 and was estimated to be '110' in 2015, what would be the country's real GDP in 2015, measured in constant 2014 dollars? [2m]

Let the country's real GDP in 2015, measured in constant 2014 dollars be 'T'.

$(136/110) = (T/100)$

Solving for T, T = $(136/110)$ X 100

= 123.6 billion

i) If the country's workers and firms operating abroad produced and earned $10 billion while the workers and firms of other countries operating within the nation produced and earned $5 billion in 2015, what would be the nominal Gross National Product (GNP) for the country that year? [2m]

Nominal GNP = Nominal GDP + net income from abroad

= 136 + (10 – 5)

= $141 billion

Answers and explanations to questions in Part 2

Question 4

a) Calculate the number of workers unemployed in 2012 and 2014. [2m]

Number of workers unemployed = Labour Force – Total Employment

For 2012, Number of workers unemployed = 24.4 – 22.2

= 2.2 million

For 2014, Number of workers unemployed = 25.6 – 21.6

= 4 million

b) Find out the rate of unemployment as a percentage for 2012 and 2014. [4m]

Rate of unemployment = Number of workers unemployed/Labour Force
X 100%

For 2012, Rate of unemployment = 2.2/24.4 X 100%

= 9%

For 2014, Rate of unemployment = 4/25.6 X 100%

= 15.6%

c) If there were 400 000 job vacancies in 2014, what would be the most likely type of unemployment in the country? Explain your answer. [4m]

In 2014, there are 4 million people unemployed and 400000 job vacancies. This means that the total structural and frictional unemployment is around 400000 and even if all the job vacancies were taken up, there would still be 3.6 million people left unemployed. Therefore, it is most likely that the type of unemployment in the country would be demand deficient or cyclical unemployment.

Answers and explanations to questions in Part 2

Question 5

a) What would be Bill and Charles' marginal rate of income tax?   [4m]

   Bill's marginal rate of income tax = 20%

   Charles' marginal rate of income tax in = 60%

b) Calculate the tax that Adam, Bill and Charles each have to pay if all of them decide to work in Country X.   [6m]

   Adam does not have to pay any tax as his annual income falls below $15000.

   Tax paid by Bill = (0% X 15000) + (10% X 10000) + (20% X 5000)

   $\qquad$ = 1000 + 1000

   $\qquad$ = $2000

   Tax paid by Charles = (0% X 15000) + (10% X 10000) + (20% X 10000) +
   $\qquad\qquad$ (30% X 10000) + (40% X 10000) + (50% X 10000) +
   $\qquad\qquad$ (60% X 20000)

   $\qquad$ = $27000

c) What are Bill and Charles' average income tax rate in country X?   [2m]

   Bill's average tax rate in country X = 2000/30000 X 100%

   $\qquad\qquad$ = 6.67%

   Charles' average tax rate in country X = 27000/85000 X 100%

   $\qquad\qquad$ = 31.7%

d) Taking into account all the information above, calculate the percentage of income paid in tax for Adam, Bill and Charles if they decide to work in Country X.

[9m]

VAT paid by Adam = 18% X (50% X $10000)

= $900

Thus, percentage of income paid in tax for Adam is 9%, since he does not pay any income tax.

VAT paid by Bill = 18% X (60% X $30000)

= $3240

Percentage of income paid in tax for Bill = (3240 + 2000)/30000 X 100%

= 17.5%

VAT paid by Charles = 18% X (45% X $85000)

= $6885

Percentage of income paid in tax for Charles = (6885 + 27000)/85000 X 100%

= 39.9%

e) If the income tax system in Country X changes so that everyone pays 25% tax regardless of income, and VAT becomes 20%, will the Gini coefficient for the country be larger or smaller than before? [6m]

Tax paid by Adam = (25% X $10000) + [20% X (50% X $10000)]

= 2500 + 1000

= 3500

Percentage of income paid in tax for Adam = 3500/10000 X 100%

= 35%

Tax paid by Bill = (25% X $30000) + [20% X (60% X $30000)]

= 7500 + 3600

= 11100

Percentage of income paid in tax for Bill = 11100/30000 X 100%

= 37%

Tax paid by Charles = (25% X $85000) + [20% X (45% X $85000)]

= 21250 + 7650

= 28900

Percentage of income paid in tax for Charles = 28900/85000 X 100%

= 34%

Since the percentage of income paid in tax increased more significantly for people who have a lower income and instead decreased for people who have a higher income, the Gini coefficient for the country will be larger than before as the income gap will widen even more with a tax system that is more regressive.

<u>Question 6</u>

a) Calculate a weighted price index for 2011. [4m]

$$\text{Weighted price index} = \frac{100 \times [\text{Sum of (Price X Weight in 2011)}]}{[\text{Sum of (Price X Weight in base year)}]}$$

$$= \frac{100 \times (128.75 + 0.5 + 3.125 + 0.015 + 0.16875 + 0.9375)}{(125 + 0.5 + 3.75 + 0.0125 + 0.125 + 0.875)}$$

$$= 133.5/130.15 \times 100$$

$$= 102.6$$

b) Calculate the average percentage increase in prices from 2010 to 2011. [2m]

Total Prices for 2010 = 500 + 2 + 30 + 0.1 + 1 + 7

= 540.1

Total Prices for 2011 = 515 + 2 + 25 + 0.12 + 1.35 + 7.5

= 551.0

Percentage increase in prices from 2010 to 2011 = (551 − 540.1)/540.1 X 100%

= 2.02%

c) Explain the difference in your answer for (a) and (b) for the year 2011. [2m]

The average percentage increase is less than the weighted change because some items (with a greater weightage) which are more widely bought have increased in prices by more than the average.

d) If Alex spent $2000 on this sample of products in 2010, how much would he spend to buy the same sample of products in 2011?   [2m]

Alex will now spend $2000 X (102.6/100) = $2052

e) Calculate the percentage change in his real income between 2011 and 2012.   [3m]

Bryan's real income will decrease by the percentage in which the price of product A increased from 2011 to 2012.

This is equal to 5/515 X 100% = 0.97%

Bryan's real income will decrease by 0.97%.

f) If Bryan's real income in 2011 was represented by an index of 100, calculate the index (to the nearest whole number) that would represent his real income in 2012.   [2m]

The index of Bryan's real income for 2012 would be 99 indicating the 0.97% decrease.

Answers and explanations to questions in Part 2

Question 7

a) Which year is the base year? [1m]

The base year is 2009 because RPI = 100

b) Calculate the rate of inflation for 2011. [2m]

Inflation for 2011 = percentage increase in RPI

= (103/101) X 100

= 101.98

Thus, rate of inflation = 2%

c) In which year did Country X face the highest rate of inflation? [2m]

The highest rate of inflation occurred in 2009 as seen in the largest percentage increase in RPI from 2008 to 2009 of 3/97 X 100% = 3.1%

d) Were prices in 2008 higher than in 2015? Explain your answer. [2m]

No, because the RPI index has decreased from 97 to 93.

e) Is Country X suffering from inflation, deflation or dis-inflation from 2011 to 2015? Explain your answer. [2m]

Country X is suffering from deflation as the RPI index has fallen from 103 in 2011 to 93 in 2015, indicating that prices have fallen.

a) What is the equilibrium price and quantity in the above market?   [2m]

From the diagram, it can be seen that the equilibrium price and quantity are $100 per tonne and 20 000 tonnes respectively.

i) Copy the diagram above and make the necessary changes to reflect the entry of foreign suppliers into the German steel market.   [2m]

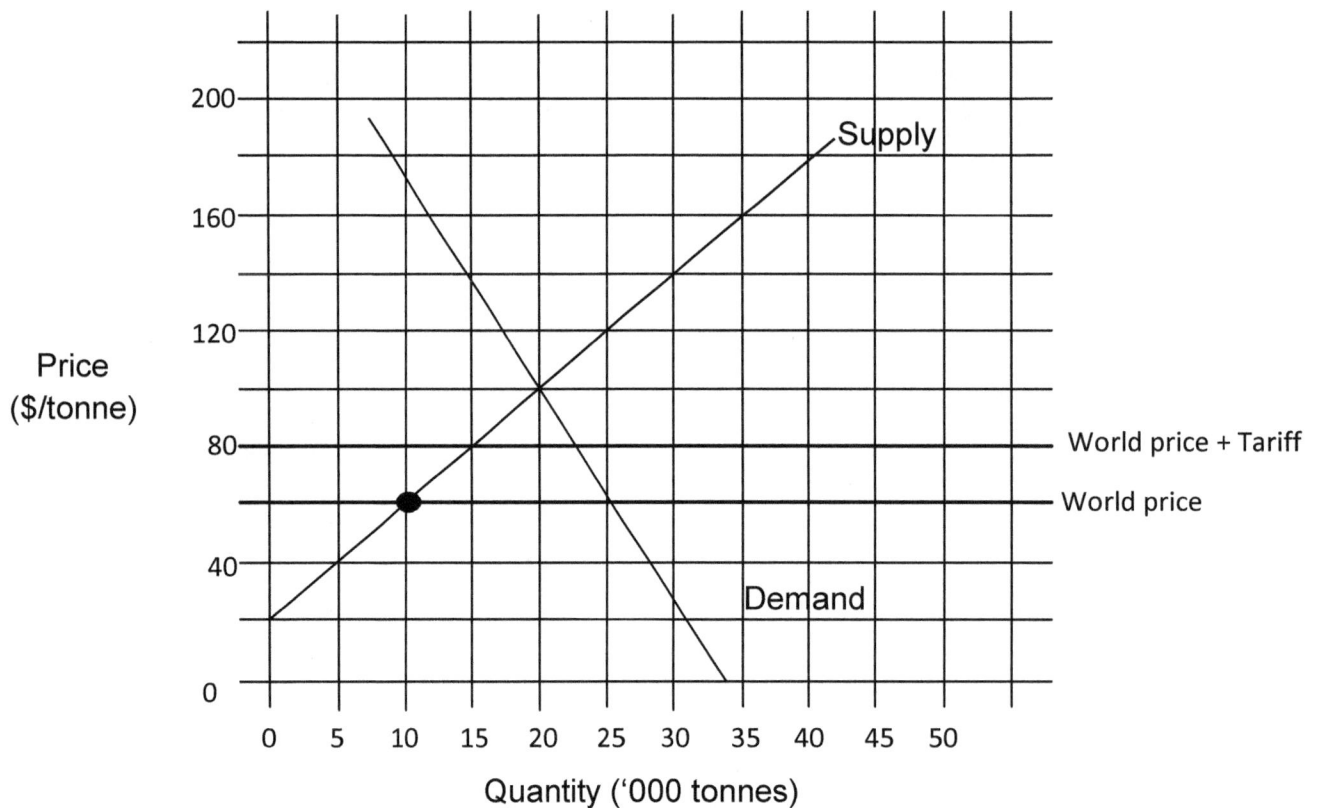

b) ii) What would be the new equilibrium price and quantity at which steel is sold in Germany when foreign steel is made available for sale in the country?

[2m]

From the new diagram in part (bi), the new equilibrium price and quantity are $60 per tonne and 25000 tonnes respectively.

c) i) How have the revenues of the domestic steel producers been affected by the entry of imported steel? Using the diagram drawn in part (bii), compare their revenue before and after free trade was permitted. [4m]

Before the entry of imported steel, German steel producers earned,

Equilibrium Price X Equilibrium Quantity = $100 X 20000 = $2000000

After free trade was permitted, they only earn,

World Price X Q_s at World Price (as seen from the diagram above)

= $60 X 10000 = $600000

Hence, the revenues of the domestic steel producers were reduced by

$2000000 − $600000 = $1400000

ii) How much revenue are the foreign steel suppliers earning from the local steel buyers in Germany? [2m]

Foreign steel suppliers are earning,

World Price X Q_s by the foreign steel suppliers
 (Q_d from the local steel buyers –
Q_s by domestic steel producers)

= $60 X (25000 – 10000) = $900000

d) How has the producer surplus been affected by the entry of the imported steel? Calculate the producer surplus before and after free trade was made available. [2m]

Initial producer surplus = 0.5 X 20000 X (100 – 20)

= $800000

Final producer surplus = 0.5 X 10000 X (60 – 20)

= $200000

The producer surplus has fallen by $600000

e) Reflect the tariff on the diagram drawn in part (bi) and find the new equilibrium price and quantity. [3m]

From the amended diagram in part (bi), the new equilibrium price and quantity are $80 per tonne and 22500 tonnes respectively.

f) Determine the revenue for the government from the tariff they implemented.

[2m]

Revenue for the government = Price of Tariff X Quantity imported

= $20 X (22500 – 15000)

= $150000

g) Find the additional revenue earned by the domestic German steel producers and thus calculate the loss in revenue by the foreign steel suppliers in the German steel market.

[4m]

Domestic German steel producers were earning $600000 before the tariff as seen part (ci).

After the tariff, they are earning $80 X 15000 = $1200000.

Hence, there is an increase of $600000 in their revenue.

Foreign steel suppliers were earning $900000 as seen in part (cii).

After the tariff, they are earning $60 X 7500 = $450000.

Thus, there is a decrease of $450000 in their revenue.

(Note: As a result of the tariff, the local steel buyers are currently paying $80 per tonne, but only the domestic steel producers are receiving $80 per tonne as $20 tariff is imposed on per tonne of imported steel)

h) Copy the original diagram and model the impact of the quota above. [2m]

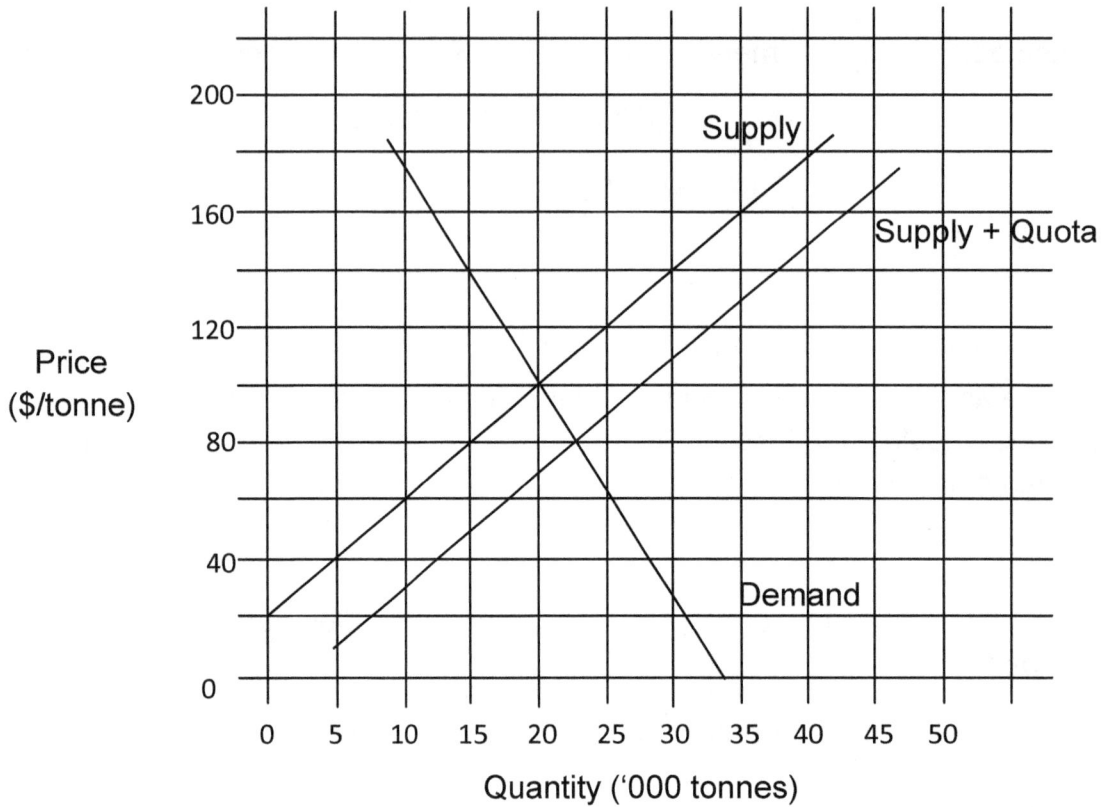

i) What would be the new equilibrium price and quantity after the imposition of the import quota? [2m]

From the diagram, the new equilibrium price and quantity are $80 per tonne and 22500 tonnes respectively.

j) i) With the quota in place, how much steel would the German producers be able to sell? What is the new revenue of the foreign steel suppliers?   [3m]

The German producers would be able to sell 15000 tonnes of steel.

The revenue of the foreign steel suppliers will now be

7500 X $80 = $600000

ii) Why have the revenues of the foreign steel producers not been reduced as much as compared to the case when the tariff was implemented?   [2m]

This is because they were able to take advantage of the higher prices that have resulted from the imposition of the quota, and collect the full $80 per tonne from the German consumers.

On the other hand, when a tariff was implemented, the additional $20 per tonne from the consumers went to the government.

Question 2

a) Taking 2007 as the base year, fill in the remaining columns for the table above.

[6m]

To calculate the index for each year, we take the price in that year, divide it by the base year price and multiply by 100.

For example, in 2006 the Index of iron ore price is (120/140) X 100 = 85.7

And in 2008, the Index will be (130/140) X 100 = 92.8, and so on.

For the Index of Iron Ore Production, it is similarly calculated as the production in one year divided by production in base year and multiplied by 100.

For the year 2009, the iron ore production index is (6.2/7.2) X 100 = 86.1 and so on.

Year	Price of Iron Ore ($ per tonne)	Index of Iron Ore Price	Iron Ore Production and Export (million tonnes)	Index of Iron Ore Production	Index of Import Prices
2005	110	78.6	6	83.3	90
2006	120	85.7	6.5	90.3	95
2007	140	100	7.2	100	100

128

2008	130	92.8	7.5	104.2	106
2009	180	128.6	6.2	86.1	110
2010	190	135.7	6.8	94.4	112

b) Find out the value of Country X's exports in 2005 and 2009.   [2m]

Value of exports = (Price per tonne of iron ore) X (Volume of iron ore produced)

Value of exports in 2005 = $110 X 6 million

= $660 million

Value of exports in 2009 = $180 X 6.2million

= $1116 million

c) Calculate the Terms of Trade (ToT) for Country X from 2005 to 2010.   [5m]

ToT = (Index of export prices X 100) / Index of import prices

For 2005, ToT = (78.6 X 100) / 90

$\qquad$ = 87.34

For 2006, ToT = (65.7 X 100) / 95

$\qquad$ = 90.21

For 2007, since the Index of Export and Import prices are equal, the ToT will be 100.

For 2008, ToT = (92.8 X 100) / 106

$\qquad$ = 87.55

For 2009, ToT = (128.6 X 100) / 110

$\qquad$ = 116.9

For 2010, ToT = (135.7 X 100) / 112

$\qquad$ = 112.2

d) Describe the trend in the ToT from 2005 to 2010. [2m]

The ToT has generally improved with the exception of 2008 where the ToT fell from 100 to 87.55.

e) If the total import expenditure in 2005 was $530 million, calculate the value of Country X's net exports. [2m]

Net exports = Value of Exports – Value of Imports

= $660 million – $530 million

= $130 million

f) If the balance of net exports calculated in part (e) is 30% of GDP, find the GDP for Country X. [2m]

GDP = ($130 million / 30) X 100

= $433 million

Question 3

a) i) Which country's currency depreciated between 2010 and 2015?   [1m]

The € currency has depreciated against the $.

ii) Find the depreciation of the currency as a percentage.   [2m]

Depreciation = (1.75 – 1.53) / 1.75 X 100

= 12.6%

b) If an IPhone 6 costs $1200 in 2015, how much would it cost in €?   [2m]

Cost in € = $1200 / 1.53

= €784

c) What would then be the equilibrium exchange rate of € in terms of $?   [3m]

Letting Qd = Qs, we have

10000 – 3000P = 2500 + 2000P

7500 = 5000P

P = 1.5

Thus, the exchange value of €1 would be $1.50.

d) With the exchange rate obtained in part (c), what would be the exchange rate of $ in terms of €? [2m]

Exchange rate = 1/1.5

= 0.667

Hence, the exchange rate of $ is €0.67.

e) Which currency was predicted to appreciate? By what percentage will it appreciate? [2m]

The $ currency was predicted to appreciate as in 2015, $1 will only be able to exchange for 1/1.53 = €0.65.

It is predicted to appreciate by (0.667 − 0.65) / 0.65 X 100% = 2.62%.

Question 4

a) What is the opportunity cost of producing (i) 1 unit of car, and (ii) 1 unit of textile for both countries A and B? [4m]

i) The opportunity cost for producing 1 unit of car is, 4 and 5 units of textiles for countries A and B respectively.

ii) The opportunity cost for producing 1 unit of textile is, 0.25 and 0.2 units of cars for countries A and B respectively.

b) Which country enjoys an absolute advantage in the production of (i) Cars, and (ii) Textiles? [2m]

Country A enjoys an absolute advantage in the production of cars while country B enjoys an absolute advantage in the production of textiles.

If both countries devote all their resources into producing cars, Country A can produce **220 cars**, while country B can only produce **200 cars**.

On the other hand, if both countries devote all their resources into producing textiles, Country A can produce 220 X 4 = **880 textiles**, while country B will be able to produce 200 X 5 = **1000 textiles**. (Since the opportunity cost for producing 1 unit of car is 4 and 5 units of textiles for countries A and B respectively)

c) For which good does each country enjoy a comparative advantage over the other country? [2m]

From part (a), country A has a lower opportunity cost in producing cars while country B has a lower opportunity cost in producing textiles.

Hence, country A enjoys a comparative advantage in producing cars while country B enjoys a comparative advantage in producing textiles.

d) How do your answers in parts (b) and (c) help to determine whether the 2 countries should trade with each other? [3m]

Answer in part (b) does not help to determine whether the 2 countries should trade with each other, as the basis for trade is differences in comparative advantage, regardless of whether a country has absolute advantage or not.

Answer in part (c) shows that both countries A and B have comparative advantages in different areas, and therefore they are able to maximise the efficiency of their resources by specialising in their areas of comparative advantages, exporting those goods which they have comparative advantage in and importing those goods which they do not have comparative advantage in. This will increase their total final output, in which they can then seek out a mutually beneficial terms of trade that can enable both countries to enjoy more consumption compared to being self-sufficient.

e) Calculate the total number of cars and textiles that would be produced if both countries decide to specialise completely in accordance with the principle of comparative advantage. [4m]

The principle of comparative advantage states that countries should specialise in producing goods that they have a lower opportunity cost in. Hence, country A should specialise in producing cars and produce 220 cars, while country B should specialise in producing textiles and produce 1000 textiles. The total number of cars would be 220 and the total number of textiles would be 1000.

f) If both countries wanted to be self-sufficient and did not trade, but devoted half of their resources to the production of cars and the other half to producing textiles, how much of each good could country A and B produce individually? [3m]

For country A, 110 units of cars and 440 units of textiles will be produced.

For country B, 100 units of cars and 500 units of textiles will be produced.

This gives a total of 210 units of cars and 940 units of textiles being produced in total.

g) On the grid below, draw the production possibility graphs for country A and B with appropriate axes labelled. [4m]

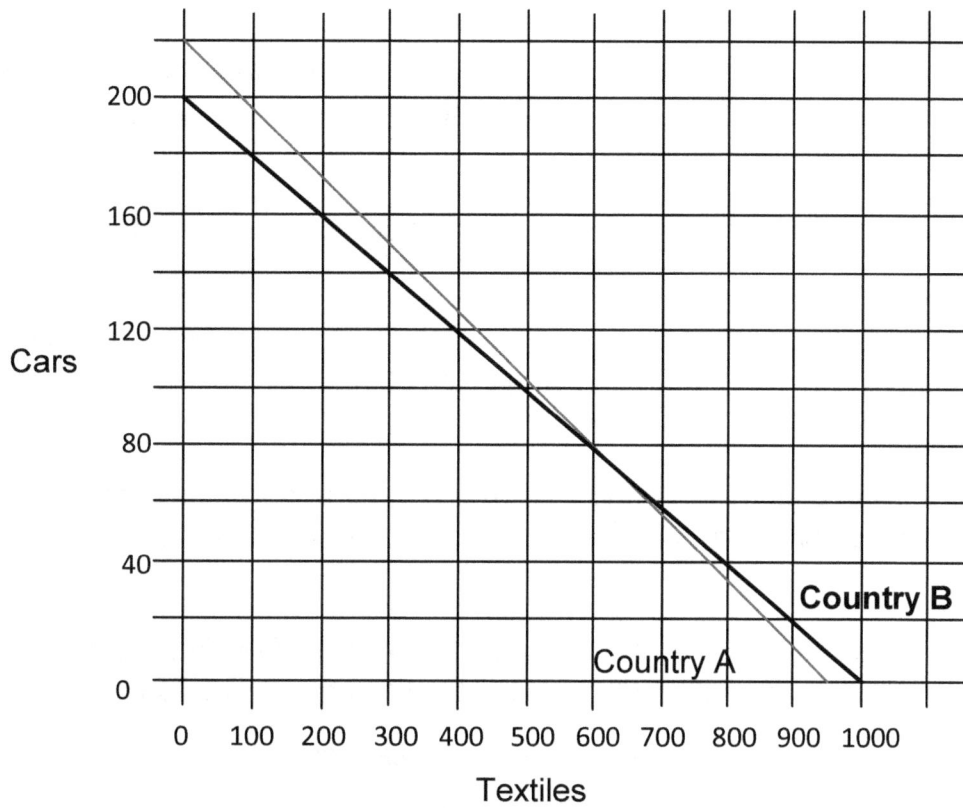

h) Assuming that Countries A and B specialise completely as in part (e), find an ideal terms of trade such that both countries would benefit and increase the total units of both their cars and textiles as compared to being self-sufficient as in part (f). [4m]

1 unit of car from country A would expect to be traded for more than 4 units of textiles and country B will not pay more than 5 units of textiles for 1 unit of car.

Hence, the terms of trade can be one unit of car for between 4 to 5 units of textiles.

One example would be country A trading 106 units of cars for 477 units of textiles from country B at an exchange rate of 1 units of car for 4.5 units of textiles.

This results in country A having 114 units of cars and 477 units of textiles, compared to having 110 units of cars and 440 units of textiles as shown in part (f).

Country B will have 106 units of cars and 523 units of textiles, compared to having 100 units of cars and 500 units of textiles as show in part (f).

Thus, this clearly shows that both countries benefited from trade and have increased consumption in both their cars and textiles.

Question 5

a) Will the devaluation of the currency have its intended effect? Explain your answer with reference to the data above.   [6m]

Devaluation of the currency would cause the exports to be cheaper in foreign currency and the imports to be more expensive in domestic currency.

Hence, the quantity demanded for imports and exports would fall and rise respectively. With a larger volume of exports and a smaller volume of imports, it seems that the balance of trade deficit can be corrected.

However, this will not actually help to correct the deficit unless the Marshall-Lerner condition ($PEDx + PEDm > 1$) holds, which is not the case here as $0.3 + 0.6 = 0.9 < 1$.

To demonstrate why does the Marshall-Lerner condition need to hold in order for the current account deficit to be corrected, let us look at the effect of the devaluation of the currency on the exports:

With the devaluation of Country's A currency by 20%, the price of exports would also fall by 20% in terms of foreign currencies for the foreign countries.

The PED of exports is 0.3, and thus the export volumes would rise by   0.3 X 20 = 6% (as PED = % change in quantity demanded / % change in price).

Hence, export revenue would increase to $9000 X 1.06 = $9540 in terms of domestic currency.

A 20% devaluation of the currency would also cause the import prices to increase by 25% in terms of domestic currency. (A devaluation of 20% would push the value of the local currency from 1 foreign currency unit down to 0.8 foreign currency units. Thus, it would take 1.25 local currency units to exchange for 1 foreign currency unit).

Since the PED of imports is 0.6, the import volumes would then fall by 0.6 X 25 = 15% (as PED = % change in quantity / % change in price).

Hence, the import expenditure of country A would be 0.85 X 10000 = $8500, measured in the original local currency and $8500 X 1.25 = $10625, measured in the new devalued currency.

From the above calculations, we can see that the trade deficit has become 10625 − 9540 = $1085, which has worsened from the initial $1000.

b) Using calculations to support your answer, show that the devaluation would have a different effect if the PED of imports and exports were both 0.8.

[4m]

In this case, the trade balance should have improved as the Marshall-Lerner condition (PEDx + PEDm > 1) would now hold as 0.8 + 0.8 = 1.6 > 1.

Export volumes would rise by 0.8 X 20 = 16%, as their prices will fall by 20% in terms of foreign currency (since PED = % change in quantity / % change in price). Thus, the export revenue would now rise to 9000 X 1.16 = $10440, in terms of domestic currency.

Similarly, the prices of imports would still rise by 25%, and the import volume would fall by 0.8 X 25 = 20% (as PED = % change in quantity / % change in price). Hence, the import expenditure of country A would fall to 0.8 X 10000 = $8000, measured in the original local currency and $8000 X 1.25 = $10000, measured in the new devalued currency.

With that, the previous $1000 current account deficit has been turned into a $440 current account surplus. Indeed, if the Marshall-Lerner condition holds, the devaluation of currency would improve the trade balance.

Question 6

a) Calculate the following,

    1) The balance of trade in goods.   [2m]

        Balance of trade = Exports of goods – Imports of goods

                = 160 – 100

                = 60 billion

    2) The balance of trade in services, income and current transfers.   [3m]

        Balance of trade in services = Exports of services – Imports of services

                        = 4 – 30

                        = – 26 billion

        Balance of income =   Income from   –   Payments to
                    foreign sources   foreign beneficiaries

                    = 2 – 16

                    = – 14 billion

        Balance of   =   Current transfers   –   Current transfers
       current transfers   from foreign sources   to foreign beneficiaries

                    = 2 – 10

                    = – 8 billion

        Hence, the balance of trade in services, income and current transfers will be (– 26 – 14 – 8 = – 48 billion)

3) The overall current account balance.   [2m]

Overall account balance = Balance of trade in goods + Balance of trade in services

$$= 60 - 48$$

$$= 12 \text{ billion}$$

4) The balance in the financial account.   [2m]

Balance in the financial account = $(6 - 0) + (0 - 12)$

$$= -6 \text{ billion}$$

b) Which of the above entries in the accounts would likely be affected by the presence of the large multinational company? Explain your answer.   [3m]

Imports of services would likely be higher as often local subsidiaries employ the financial and marketing services of the head office which would be located back in the home country.

Direct investment from foreign sources would likely be higher as the multinational would regularly invest capital from its home country in local operations.

Current transfers to foreign beneficiaries would likely be higher as the foreign technicians and managers working for the multinational would send remittances to their home countries.

www.ingramcontent.com/pod-product-compliance
Lightning Source LLC
Chambersburg PA
CBHW062027210326
41519CB00060B/7186